Thomas Battye

A Disclosure of Parochial Abuse, Artifice and Peculation in the town of Manchester

Thomas Battye

A Disclosure of Parochial Abuse, Artifice and Peculation in the town of Manchester

ISBN/EAN: 9783337146108

Printed in Europe, USA, Canada, Australia, Japan

Cover: Foto ©ninafisch / pixelio.de

More available books at **www.hansebooks.com**

A DISCLOSURE

of

Parochial Abuse, Artifice, & Peculation,

in the Town of

MANCHESTER;

which have been the Means of burthening the Inhabitants
with the present

ENORMOUS PARISH RATES:

with

other existing

IMPOSITIONS OF OFFICE,

IN A VARIETY OF FACTS,

exhibiting

the cruel and inhuman Conduct

of the

HIRELING OFFICERS OF THE TOWN,

towards the

P O O R.

To which is added,

A BOOK OF COUNTY RATES,

shewing

the exact Proportion of every HUNDRED IN THIS County,
and of every *Township in the Hundred of Salford.*

BY THOMAS BATTYE.

SECOND EDITION.

" If a long train of abuses, peculation, and artifices, all tending the same way, make the
" design visible to the inhabitants, and they cannot but feel what they lie under, and see
" whither they are going; it is not to be wondered, that they should then rouse themselves
" and endeavour to put the management into such hands, as may secure to them the ends,
" for which parochial offices were first appointed."

SOLD BY J. THOMSON, MARKET-STREET-LANE,

Manchester.

1796.

A DISCLOSURE, &c.

The importance of the subject to the inhabitants of the town of Manchester, which an enquiry into the conduct of its officers involved, might have been deemed sufficient to preclude the necessity of any prefatory observations; but as it may appear rather extraordinary, that an individual should obtrude himself, as I have done, upon the public attention, it may not be altogether improper to state, that had I experienced that *liberality, candour*, and *love of justice*, which is so much the favourite topic of *some men*'s professions, and so *little* the subject of their actions and proceedings, this publication would not have made its appearance. It was with a view to disclose to the inhabitants a scene of *abuse, artifice*, and *peculation*, practised in the township, that I first excited this investigation; and though many obstacles have been thrown in my way, by those who should have countenanced the proceeding, yet they have not deterred me from prosecuting my original design. The information conveyed in the following pages, was intended to have been submitted to the consideration of the public, through the medium of a town's meeting; therefore, if any apology be necessary for the mode in which it is now brought forward, it is due from those gentlemen who so unaccountably obstructed the regular and intended course of enquiry.

B

When

When the business was first agitated at the Bull's-head, the opinion of the town was evidently and decidedly for an investigation into *abuses*, known to exist in its civil regulations. At that meeting, the *long lost book*, called the *Red Basil*, was brought forward to public view, with a balance in favour of the town of THREE THOUSAND THREE HUNDRED AND SIX POUNDS SEVENTEEN SHILLINGS AND SIX-PENCE! The few charges adduced at the meeting, were established by the concurrent evidence of several witnesses, while the *prevaricating* and *shuffling counter testimony* of Mr. Hallows, with *his story of his friend the poll-davy weaver*, and his *" dusty shelf,"* flashed conviction into the minds of every person present. Indeed *all* seemed to manifest a zealous wish to prosecute the enquiry, and to heal those cancerous and corroding parts in the system; which *ignorance, mismanagement, peculation,* and *breach of trust had engendered!* It seldom, if ever, happens, that public opinion, fairly and impartially taken, errs in judgment; such was the case in the present enquiry, which appeared from the decided approbation given to the proposed measure. I should be wholly at a loss after this, to account for that *subsequent* opposition given by certain individuals in its progress, did I not sufficiently know to what absurd lengths the spirit of *party* leads, and the gratification it feels from *opposition*—even to measures of *public good.*

It will not be improper in this place to observe, that by the advertisement of the Boroughreeve and Constables of the 9th Nov. 1794, the charges against Mr. Unite (which appeared in a paragraph in the Chester paper) *" were conceived to be " of considerable magnitude, and worthy the most " minute investigation; that they then called upon*
the

" the Author to substantiate his charges, if true, that
" justice might be done to the public by the immediate
" dismissal of Mr. Unite from his office, or otherwise
" that he might come forward and PUBLICLY
" exculpate himself *from so foul an accusation.*"

Upon avowing myself the Author of the paragraph alluded to in the above advertisement, a
public meeting was convened on the 26th of the
same month, to hear Mr. Unite's defence, when
the following resolutions were entered into.

Bull's-head, Nov. 26, 1794.

THOMAS RICHARDSON, Esq. in the Chair.

Resolved,

1st, That it is the opinion of this meeting, that
Mr. Unite's conduct, during the time he served
the office of Overseer and Deputy Constable of
the Township of *Manchester*, shall undergo a *general investgation.*

After some progress in the investigation of the
said charges, it was resolved,

2dly, That a committee of twelve should be
appointed to investigate the nature and particulars of a certain book, called the "*Red Basil Book,*"
then produced ; and also to investigate the *general conduct* of Mr. Unite, during the period he
was in the offices of *Overseer* and *Deputy Constable* of the Town of *Manchester,* and that such
committee should report the result of their investigation *to an adjournment of this meeting.*

3dly, That any five of the said committee
should be competent to act.

4thly, That the said committee should consist
of the following gentlemen, viz. Mr. James
Smith, Mr. Seddon, Mr. A. Clegg, Mr. Farrand,
Mr.

Mr. Routh, Mr. Lloyd, Mr. Bingham, Mr. C.
Rider, Mr. Branch, Mr. Thomas Preston, Mr.
J. Hurst, and Mr. Roberts.

5thly, That the unanimous thanks of the meeting should be given to the Chairman, for his very
FAIR and IMPARTIAL conduct on this occasion,
*and also to the Constables, for their attention to this
business.*

5thly, That the meeting should be adjourned,
to be held at the call of the Boroughreeve and
Constables.

After a very *long* and *laborious enquiry,* in pur-
suance of the above resolutions, in the course of
which I *produced evidence to substantiate my charges,*
the *Boroughreeve* and *Constables were requested by
the* COMMITTEE *to call a town's meeting, agreeably
to the last resolution, to receive their* REPORT.

But what must be the astonishment excited in
the mind of every thinking and impartial person,
to find this requisition *refused,* and on a plea the
most *frivolous* and *groundless,* as appears by the
following extract of their letter on the 4th March
last, inserted in the public papers, " that *a public*
" *meeting cannot with any degree of EFFECT or*
" *PROPRIETY be called for the purpose expressed*
" *in your (the committee's) requisition, for it is ev-*
" *ident that such a meeting could not be competent,*
" *either to ACQUIT Mr. Unite, if INNOCENT,*
" *or PUNISH him, if GUILTY!* Can any man,
possessed of common understanding, read this
new declaration of the *Boroughreeve* and *Constables*
without astonishment; or by any means reconcile
it to the purport of their former letter of the 9th
November 1794? Did not these gentlemen, at
the public meeting, held on the 26th of the same
month, conceive, that if the charges against Mr.
Unite could have been conveniently investigated,
and the sense of the inhabitants taken, that they
would

would have been bound by the determination of that meeting? If not, why was such a meeting called? Why did *they themselves* propose a committee of investigation, if no attention were to be paid to the result of it? Why was I put to a very considerable expence in bringing evidence before the committee, to substantiate my charges against Mr. Unite, if the public must be deprived of the benefit?

Let no pretence of *party (which I totally disclaim)* be an obstacle to the public good. For my own part, I cannot help considering the refusal of the Boroughreeve and Constables to carry into effect the resolutions of a town's meeting, a proceeding of a very *curious complexion;* and I am at a loss to discover from whence they derive an authority, thus to put a *negative* on the *public* will. What! have the inhabitants of this town no *right* or *power* to enquire into its *abuses,* and into the *conduct of its servants?* Are they quietly to witness *enormities* and *abuses* that disgrace its civil regulations, *without a liberty to investigate and remove them?* I declare I know not which would be the more glaring, the *impudence* and *absurdity* of such a declaration, or the blameable and injurious apathy and inattention the public would manifest by neglecting to assert and exercise this its *acknowledged* and *most important privilege.* We are surely not so totally unacquainted with the laws of our country, as to be ignorant that a town's meeting is neither competent to *acquit innocence,* or *convict guilt, in a judicial capacity!* The nature and object of the intended meeting was *not* that it should *there* and *then* exercise the functions of a *Jury,* or *Court of Justice,* but simply those of an *Accuser* and *Prosecutor,* if ground of accusation had been established. Mr. Unite, as a servant to the town of Manchester,

was

was clearly amenable to the public for any impropriety of conduct in his office. It was for a town's meeting to decide, on the charges brought against him, and to have determined in consequence, either to have *dismissed him* for *neglect*, or *inattention*—to have punished him in a court of justice, if guilty of *peculation*, or *breach of trust*, or, if *innocent* and *blameless*, to have continued towards him its support and patronage. But Mr. Unite in his advertisement, *impudently* asserts— " that the *public* are *incompetent to judge of his con- " duct*," and pretends to "*challenge and court an " investigation by law !"* But will the *Boroughreeve* and *Constables* undertake, at the *town's expence*, to support such a prosecution, if instituted, or will they *defend it?*

If Mr. Unite had indeed been clothed in the impenetrable "*armour of innocence*" he speaks of, what could he possibly have to fear from any enquiry into his conduct, at a town's meeting? Conscious that every lance must have glanced harmless, he would surely have been proud and wishful of an opportunity to vindicate his character, assured of the *triumph* that must in that case have awaited its investigation? Why, thus doubly shielded with *innocence* and *codt of mail*, he should have *shrunk* from the proposed enquiry, it is not for me to decide. *Innocence* loves and courts the light, it is *guilt* alone that shuns the face of day, and flies into caverns of darkness for concealment. But to come more immediately to the subject in question.

At this time, the most serious attention of *every Ley Payer* is requisite, to *reduce*, or at least, as much as possible to *prevent* the increase of the very heavy and accumulating burthens, which the inhabitants of *Manchester* lie under.

On the perusal of the following sheets, the
public

public will cease from surprise at the disbursements, of this township having encreased since
the year 1790, from EIGHT THOUSAND to
upwards of TWENTY THOUSAND POUNDS
per annum!!

.. I shall now proceed to lay before the public
some part of the evidence I brought before the
committee; and that it may appear as little tedious as possible to the reader, I shall *only* insert
one or *two* instances under each of the *various*
classes of *abuse* !

- The RED BASIL BOOK, produced at the
Meeting at the Bull's-head, on the 26th Nov.
1794, is entitled "An exact account of
"the arrears in bastardy, from *May*
" 1773, to *February* 1787," which amounts to
THREE THOUSAND THREE HUNDRED
AND SIX POUNDS SEVENTEEN SHIL-
LINGS AND SIX-PENCE. This register was
first formed by Mr. Beaumont, the late overseer
of the poor, from other books in his possession,
the balance of which is calculated up to the latter
date, Feb. 1787; and *which arrears must have*
been progressively accumulating since that period.
This book seems deficient, in not stating the pre-
cise time the debts became due ; and it is likewise impossible to state what amount was received
by Mr. Beaumont in his life, as the committee
appointed to investigate Mr. Unite's conduct, *was*
not able to procure an inspection of his BOOKS and
PAPERS, which appear to have been regularly
delivered to him as successor to Mr. Beaumont.
In this Book, there are *Twelve Hundred and*
Twenty-eight persons mentioned, and it is rather
extraordinary that Mr. Edgely should have only
received from Mr. Unite two hundred and ninety-
three orders of filiation, which orders are necessary
to enforce the payment of the arrears. Will any
man,

man, possessed of common understanding, suppose that *all* the bastardy accounts, which appear posted up to Feb. 1787, could have been closed by Mr. Beaumont in two years? If the public are credulous enough to believe that *all* the children belonging to *Six Hundred and Fourteen Fathers*, or the children born since the year 1787, died before the year 1790, I shall then admit, that the RED BASIL BOOK was of no use, but justly closed at the death of Mr. Beaumont.

It is likewise somewhat extraordinary that this register should have been delivered to Mr. *Hallows*, when it was the *appointed department of Mr. Edgley* to keep *these accounts!* It appears that Mr. Edgley has kept the *bastardy accounts* since July 1790, when he applied to Mr. Unite for *all* the *accounts in his possession,* but never saw the Red Basil Book before the meeting at the Bull's-head, nor ever knew that Mr. Hallows was in possession of it; that he heard some months after he came into office, in the year 1790, that there was such a book; but that he *never saw any regular accounts of* BASTARDY MONEY *before he came into office!* so that there does not appear any regular *register* of *illegitimacy kept from the year 1787 to the year 1790, nor any balance to have been received from Mr. Unite when he quitted the office of overseer!* Mr. Edgley has justly observed, that this book would have been of infinite service to him in the keeping of these accounts, for that he experienced much inconvenience from the circumstance of only receiving from Mr. Unite, when he came into office, A FEW LOOSE SHEETS OF PAPER!!

Well might Mr. Edgley make this complaint on the irregularity of his predecessor's conduct, in furnishing him only with scattered and confused

sheets

sheets of paper, which, instead of elucidating, must have involved him in doubt and obscurity, and afforded him no clue whatever to the nature and duties of his new office. In short, they might justly be compared to the faint glimmerings of our thinly-scattered police lamps, which serve only to make "*darkness visible,*" and to bewilder, where they should guide and direct.

Mr. Edgley, however, soon finding these illegitimate concerns to encrease on his hands, very properly opened a new set of books, for the express purpose of recording these transactions; *the begetting of bastards, seems to have been a part of the parish* business, totally unknown to Mr. Unite, *as overseer.*

By the minutes taken at the Bull's-head meeting, by Messrs. Milne and Sergeant, it appears by the testimony of Mr. Hallows, that he did not receive the Red Book in question, till three months after he came into office, that he afterwards *wisely* called in his friend Leyland, *the polldavy weaver,* to assist him in the examination of it, when their united opinion judged it not worth *Five Shillings! This, Mr. Hallows says, was his only reason, for keeping it so long* upon his " *dusty " shelf;*" but if I may be allowed to differ from these gentlemen in opinion, I should think it a cheap purchase at *Five Hundred Guineas,* to have it regularly transferred, with its necessary vouchers, and security given to have such sums of money returned *as may appear to have been collected,* and by MISTAKE *unentered!*

The account given by Mrs. Hallows, relative to the delivery of this book, agrees with that given by her husband, except that it was delivered some time after the other books. That she thought *the reason of its then being brought* was, that Mrs. Beaumont, widow of the late overseer, had ex-

pressed

pressed some doubts to Mr. Hallows, as to the propriety of Mr. Unite's keeping the book, and receiving monies from it. And that Mr. Hallows was greatly distressed when he came into office, for *want of the proper* BOOKS *and* PAPERS *being delivered to him.*

The notes extracted from the Red Book, can by no means be said to constitute its value, though Mr. Unite positively asserted, that Mr. Beaumont sent for him to Eccles, when he was on his death-bed, to tell him *that the Red Basil Book was of no use whatever.:* yet there appears to be the names of many persons of property and respectability, from whom a considerable sum might be collect-ed, if it had not already been received, of which I can find no account in the book. It is like-wise very improbable that Mr. Hallows, and his friend Leyland, should form such an opinion, that the book was of no value, for it evidently ap-pears that some persons must have thought dif-ferently, or they would not have taken the trouble *to foist in a deceptive alteration,* which is a con-vincing proof that it had not entirely been *un-noticed.* It likewise appears that Mr. Unite had received *many sums* of money from persons named therein, that he called upon a gentleman in the neighbourhood of *Manchester, who paid him the amount of the balance therein specified, which sum of money Mr. Unite has not accounted for!*

Yet, in the minutes taken by Messrs. Milne and Sergeant, at the meeting at the Bull's-head, Mr. Unite declares that he never received any monies from the Red Book. Messrs. Harrop and Wheel-er, in their papers, both mention Mr. Unite to have answered every question *unequivocally,* and that he never had received a farthing from the book in question.

From the information which Mr. Hallows,

who)

(who succeeded Mr. Unite in the office of overseer) must be capable of conveying to the public,
it was thought proper to request his attendance,
but he refused to appear. The committee were induced to repeat their request, representing to him,
that he would be treated with great respect, as they
were appointed at a numerous town's meeting, to
make a particular investigation, and that it was
thought necessary to call upon him to facilitate the
same, but he again refused giving the necessary
information. It ought to be remembered, that
Mr. Hallows at that time received a salary of
ONE HUNDRED AND FIFTY POUNDS a
year, as one of the *deputy overseers of the town.*

The following examination forms a charge of
a very serious nature.

James Taylor, musician, says, that about Easter,
1789, he was employed by the church-wardens
and overseers of the poor, as an assistant to Mr.
Beaumont, the standing overseer of Manchester,
that he does not recollect, during his employment
with Mr. Beaumont, that the *Red Book was ever
omitted being brought for the inspection of the magistrates at the weekly sessions,* that it was written by
Mr. Beaumont, who calculated the arrears up to
1787, and that it was of great service to him, in
the collection of the out-standing *bastardy money,* as
he could immediately have referred to any account, having arranged them in alphabetical order;
that it was his department to visit the poor, and
report their situation ; that he continued assistant
to the said Mr. Beaumont from that time until his
death, which was about July 1790; says, that
during all the time he was assistant, when application was made to Mr. Beaumont, by poor people
belonging to other parishes, he visited them to see
whether they were sick, or in distress, and if they
were,

were, Mr. Beaumont wrote to the overseer of the parish where they belonged, and informed him of their situation, and what they earned weekly, at the same time begged to know if it were agreeable that they should be relieved, and to what extent, and if the township of Manchester would be indemnified for the same, otherwise they would be removed. The overseers in their answer, generally requested Mr. Beaumont to relieve them, as he would his own poor, holding their townships responsible for repayment. Says, Mr. Beaumont, on receipt of such answers and promised indemnity, relieved them *by an order upon the cashier, or pay-master of the town's money*, with such sums as he thought necessary, and as he from time to time specified in each order. That in relieving such poor, who were every day very numerous, Mr. Beaumont made it a *constant* and *invariable* practice to write the *parish, township,* or *place,* to which each pauper belonged, at the foot of every note, in order that the *cashier* might *debit* such *township, parish,* or *place* with the *amount of each sum paid;* that Mr. *Wharmby* was cashier the first part of the time he was assistant, and Mr. *Edgley* during the latter, *and that it was agreed and perfectly understood among them, that when the* PARISH, TOWNSHIP, *or* PLACE, to which the persons sent to be relieved, *was not inserted in the note, they were in that case understood by the cashier to belong to Manchester.* Says, when Mr. Beaumont was either going himself, or sending him, this examinant, any journey into the country, *about removals, or bastardy warrants,* or upon any town's business, the cashier was previously applied to for the account of monies owing by the respective overseers, that happened to be in or near the rout of their intended journey, which was always made out, and the money collected accordingly.

Says,

Says, when Mr. Beaumont sent him, this examinant, any journey on the town's business, he always required the particulars of the expences in writing, which were regularly noted. Says, that after the death of Mr. Beaumont, this examinant continued for some time the practice of relieving the poor belonging to other places, by inserting the *parish, township*, or *place*, to which they respectively belonged, at the *bottom of each note,* for a short time, until it was observed by Mr. Unite, who disapproved *of the practice,* and ordered him to discontinue it, *and to tear the two notes he had just made out.* This examinant says, that he told Mr. Unite that it was Mr. Beaumont's practice, in order *that the cashier might know to what place they belonged, and to prevent* them from being entered *as* MANCHESTER POOR, to which Mr. Unite replied, " *what is it to me where they " belong, so that I keep an account of them myself." Mr. Unite then ordered this examinant to write the two notes again, and not to insert the place to which the paupers belonged; that when he had written them, Mr. Unite pulled out a small memorandum book from his pocket, and wrote down the names of the paupers, the places to which they belonged, and the sum ordered to be paid.* Says, that from the time Mr. Unite ordered him to *destroy* the notes, (which was about two months after he was appointed overseer, until he, this examinant, left his service, at Shrove-tide, 1791) he discontinued the above practice adopted by Mr. Beaumont, and also the practice of entering the particulars of the expences of each journey, and instead thereof entered *the same* in a *gross sum.* Says, he has frequently seen Mr. Unite make entries in *private memorandum books,* to which this examinant never had access. Says, after the above practice was discontinued, he, this examinant, when

any

any journey was to be taken into the country, *was never sent to Mr. Edgley for the accounts of the country overseers,* as he *very frequently had been when he was assistant to Mr. Beaumont.* That Mr. Unite afterwards gave orders, *that all persons who did not belong to Manchester, should be relieved on a particular day in every week,* (except in desperate cases) *on which day Mr. Unite generally sent this examinant out of the way, upon some frivolous errand.* This examinant further says, he was much dissatisfied. on the above occasion, and told Mr. Unite in the *board-room,* at the *workhouse,* that *he was acting dishonestly,* and that he at that time made it a constant practice to speak of Mr. Unite's conduct publicly. Says, during the time he served as assistant to Mr. Beaumont, he kept a very LARGE FOLIO LETTER BOOK, with an *alphabetical index* of *parishes* and *townships,* and a VISITING BOOK, for the purpose of entering the *situation* and *circumstances* of all persons applying for relief, and the places of their settlement; also, a NARROW CASH-BOOK; says, on the death of Mr. Beaumont, the said books came regularly into the possession of Mr. Unite, who kept them during the time of his being assistant, but not so regularly, after *a short time,* as Mr. Beaumont had done. Says, *all* LETTERS *received from country overseers were regularly preserved* during the whole time he was assistant both to Mr. Beaumont and Mr. Unite, for the purpose of *proving,* with the *assistance* of the *letter-book,* the *specific engagements* and *promises* made by such overseers, *which were in general the only vouchers to enable the town of Manchester to obtain payments of money so advanced on their account.*

This information being obtained, it was thought highly necessary to inspect these books, and application

plication was made to Mr. Hallows, as successor to Mr. Unite, to enquire after Mr. Beaumont's *letter-book*, which would have been a proper key to discover the places in correspondence with this town, and in all probability, would have led to a developement of Mr. Unite's conduct, but Mr. Hallows declared, that he had never received any such book. Mrs. Beaumont was then applied to, who recollected the book, having herself copied letters therein, and described it to be *a large bound folio book, that it was delivered to Mr. Unite, at the death of her husband, with several bundles of letters, which were folded up according to their dates, and which, with the letter-book, were the vouchers of the agreements entered into by country overseers. These letters, and the letters received by Mr. Unite, in his overseership, have never since made their appearance.*

Application was then made to Mr. Unite relative to the book, *who seemed at first not to recollect it,* when after some time, he said, *he had such a book, but that he never made use of it.* He was then asked what sort of a book it was, and his description corresponded with Mrs. Beaumont's. Upon being asked, if he was sure he never wrote in it, or made use of it, he replied, that *he might have wrote in it, but he was not certain ; he thought he wrote a letter or two, but that he had delivered it over to Mr. Hallows, with the other books.* On being asked, if he was certain of its being delivered to Mr. Hallows, he replied, *he was,* that the *books were carried away at different times.* This induced a second application to Mr. Hallows, who persisted in his former assertion of not having received the book. Mr. Hallows then sent a boy for Mr. Unite to justify his assertion. The boy returned for answer, that *Mr. Unite was going out with some warrants about the police tax.* Mr. Hallows

lows then promised to see Mr. Unite, and to call upon the committee in the afternoon. Mr. Hallows waited upon one of the gentlemen of the committee the day following, *but could not prevail upon Mr. Unite to accompany him.* The committee were now reduced to the necessity of desiring Mr. Unite to fix a time when they might make enquiry as to the above-mentioned books ; upon which Mr. Unite waited upon one of the gentlemen, who read over to him a list of the following books.

, Mr. Beaumont's *large folio letter-book, visiting-book, cash-book, bastardy-book of monies* received, and his *long narrow cash-book,* to which Mr. Unite replied, " *I have delivered them all to Mr. Hal-* " *lows.*" It was again thought necessary to apply to Mr. Hallows, for the inspection of ALL his books and papers, received from Mr. Unite. The books Mr. Hallows produced, were carefully examined, *but not* ONE *of the books in the before mentioned list, were found.* If the days of superstition and miracle were not now in their wane, we might be almost led to attribute the wonderful and sudden disappearance of these books to the effect of magic art, and to suppose they had been conjured away by the potent wand of a Prospero.

The following are some observations made on the inspection of the books found at Mr. Hallows's house.

. In one book there appears one hundred and seventy-four *examinations in bastardy,* entered by Mr. Unite, the first dated the 1st of April 1790, and the last dated the 1st of October 1791. Immediately after follow one hundred and eighty-eight entered by Mr. Hallows, the first dated the 1st of April 1792, and the last the 12th of November 1794, from which it appears that no examinations
were

were taken between the 1st of March and the 12th
of June 1792.

In the same book there are one hundred
and seventy-three *examinations for settlements*, entered by Mr. Unite, the first dated the 14th of
May 1789, and the last dated the 27th of October
1791, a period of two years and a half. After
which there appears to have been four hundred and
forty-four *examinations entered* by Mr. Hallows, the
first dated the 19th of April 1792, and the last
dated the 5th of November 1794, comprising the
same period of time, though little short of *three
times the number!* and it is somewhat remarkable,
that no examinations whatever took place between
the 27th of October and the 19th of April 1792,
a period of near SIX MONTHS!

There also appears one hundred and thirty-six
removal orders, entered by Mr. Unite in the same
book, the first bearing date the 14th of May 1789,
and the latter the 1st of March 1792, a period of
three years and a quarter. After which there appears entered by Mr. Hallows *two hundred and
twenty-seven*, the first bearing date the 12th of June
1792, and the last the 12th of December 1794 *, a
period of only *two years and a half!* in which it
appears that the *removal orders have increased* to THREE TIMES the number. The price
in obtaining these orders, has of late risen from
nine to fourteen shillings, which has made these removals worth attention. FIVE shillings are now
paid for examination, FOUR for the order, and FIVE
shillings for MOVING THE BENCH! The New
Bayley Remembrancer (which ought to be investigated) will exhibit an account of many hundred pounds paid for such like removals. On
this

D

* There appears a chasm in this book of removal orders,
of near four months, which, together with a cessation of
NEAR SIX MONTHS in the *examinations of bastardy*, appears
to be the overseers' *vacation*, not noticed by almanack-makers.

this incongruous and confused mass of circumstances, I shall only observe to the reader, that Mr. Hallows appears to have had *the management* of conducting the paupers to their places of settlement, and his *profit* on these conveyances is *immense*, as I shall hereafter point out.

In the beginning of the books for the year 1786 and 1787, and the succeeding books, it is stated by the magistrates order, that the accounts are to be kept under the following heads, viz. *Clothing, Burials, Law Expences, Apprentices, Extraordinaries, Rents,* and *incidental Expences.* Mr. Beynon's accounts from 1782 to 1787, appear all regularly kept, and also Mr. Bradbury's, both of which I find *are closed by a general cash account,* in which the *receipts* and *disbursements* are particularly specified, and a balance struck. After the year 1789 there appears no books kept in the same regular manner.

In the book, containing an account of the monies paid by the township for the maintenance of bastard children, from Easter 1787 to Easter 1788, the arrears owing by the reputed fathers of these children, *are brought forward;* but in the accounts kept by Mr. Unite of these expences, from Easter 1790 to Easter 1791, and from Easter 1791 to Easter 1792, no *notice is taken of these arrears, they are neither brought forward, when he came into office, nor is there any account of them when he quitted.* These books *only contain an account of monies* PAID by the township for the maintenance of these children, without the account of a *single shilling* RECEIVED *from the reputed fathers !* What a happy and self-satisfying mode of keeping a cash-book, where units, tens, and hundreds appear to the credit of the disburser, with nothing on the debit side to lessen and disturb the balance, but harmless ciphers.

It ought to be particularly noticed, that in these
. books

books there are a great number of PRIVATE
MARKS, in a variety of forms (not much unlike
Egyptian hieroglyphics); these are, no doubt, re-
ferences to other accounts not intended for the
inspection of the Ley-payers, and are sufficient to
raise *strong* suspicions of *secret* and *unfair* practices in this department.

In the book, which contains a register of the
certificates from other parishes, and of the bonds
of indemnity given by reputed fathers of bastard
children, it is somewhat curious, that only two certificates have of late years been entered, and the
last bond of indemnity, *to which a date is fixed*, pre-
vious to Mr. Hallows coming into office, is dated
the 7th of November 1788. Eleven are afterwards entered *without date*. There appears seven
entered by Mr. Hallows in 1792, but none in 1793,
and only three in 1794.

The regulation of the magistrates only extends
to the mode of *keeping an account of the disburse-*
ments; but the language of the act directs, that
" a *just, true*, and *perfect* account shall be kept,
fairly entered in a book for the purpose, *(not on*
slips of paper) by the churchwardens and overseers, of all sums of money by them received, or
rated and assessed, and not received, and also of
all goods and chattels, stock and materials, that
shall be in their hands, or in the hands of any of
their poor, in order to be wrought, and of all
monies paid by such churchwarden and overseer
so accounting, and of *all other* things concerning
the said office, and shall also pay and deliver
over all sums of money, goods, and chattels,
as shall be then in their hands, to the succeeding overseers;" but from a variety of facts
which this publication discloses, it is evident, that
Mr. Unite has been *culpably inattentive* to the duty
required by this act of parliament. That he received the regular books, he does not pretend to
deny;

deny; but as their public appearance at this time would discover his clandestine proceedings, he shuns the investigation under a *shuffling* pretence of having delivered them to his successor, Mr. Hallows, whom he refused to meet on that business. The *folio letter book* is said to contain *eight* or *ten* quires of paper, consequently not easily lost, and shews every agreement entered into by country overseers. *Birmingham,* a town nearly equal in size to Manchester, has no less than four hundred different accounts with the surrounding townships, though the overseers of Birmingham are not in the habit of boarding paupers belonging to other parishes, as the workhouse at that place is scarcely sufficient to contain their own poor, yet they account for betwixt THREE and FOUR HUNDRED POUNDS A YEAR *received for certificate cases* ONLY, exclusive of what is received for *orders of bastardy;* they have likewise debited themselves with the receipt of near four hundred pounds a year for *composition money,* which is in Manchester termed HUSH-MONEY. In our workhouse, it was till lately no uncommon thing to receive the poor belonging to any township, from one shilling to three shillings a head. Bed-ridden old women, and, according to Mr. Unite's account, "*wild lunatics,*" are boarded and taken every necessary care of, at *two shillings per week.* This workhouse is likewise a *receptacle for tradesmen's wives,* when they become troublesome to their husbands, who are taken in as low as four shillings per week, with every necessary accommodation.

Under a variety of such circumstances, and the cash which must be under the management of an overseer weekly, I am astonished, I must confess, that there appears no CASH BOOK kept by Mr. Unite, as overseer! nor any *debtor* and *creditor account!*

The following I have inserted, to shew the Ley-payers, the methods made use of by our overseers, by beginning with an example near home. In the overseers' books at Cheetham, there appears the following entries.

1790, April 18, Cash paid R. Unite,
on *last year's account*, for N. Milling........: 4 2 0
 Paid ditto for Scholes's wife bedding,
(out of Manchester workhouse)............... 2 13 6
 Paid ditto for board in the workhouse 0 18 0
1791, 25 April, Paid ditto nineteen
weeks, at 3s.. 2 17 0
 Paid ditto, from 25 April to June 4.... 1 10 0

          12 0 6
By cash accounted for by Mr. Unite 6 18 0

Balance in favour of the town, which
I cannot find accounted for £5 2 6

As these kind of transactions are so numerous, the recital would not only appear tedious, but would swell this into a voluminous work, I shall therefore only state another case or two, to shew that it was not only Mr. Unite's method, but was likewise practised by his successor in office.

The following transactions between *Mr. Unite, Mr. Edgley,* and *Mr. Hallows,* with the township of Radcliffe, will serve to explain the account given by Mr. Taylor, as well as the *reason* for discontinuing the method used by Mr. Beaumont.

Mr. Kay, the overseer of Radcliffe, received a few months ago a letter from Mr. Hallows, threatening *to arrest him, if he did not immediately remit him the sum of sixteen pounds two shillings, which Hallows said, was for money that* HE *had advanced Betty Allen, at one shilling and six-pence per week, for* SEVERAL YEARS, and who, he said, belonged to Radcliffe parish. The overseer, a plain shrewd man, having regularly paid *Mr. Unite and Mr.*
Edgley,

Edgley, for Betty Allen's relief, at different pay-ments, was astonished at the application, and sus-pected something unfair in this business; he there-fore set off immediately, on the receipt of Mr. Hallows's letter, to Manchester, with his books, and meeting with him at the New Bayley, shewed him his accounts with *Mr. Unite and Mr. Edgley, with their receipts annexed to each payment.* Hal-lows then told Mr. Kay, that *he had no right to have paid Mr. Edgley, as he was sure Edgley would never enter it as received.* Mr. Hallows then requested the overseer to shew him the let-ter he had received, and on his producing it, *Hallows put it hastily into his pocket, and told the overseer that it was a* MISTAKE, *that the letter was written by his* CLERK. Mr. Kay not a little cha-grined at being put to the trouble and expence of this journey, added to the manner in which the let-ter was taken from him, then made application to Mr. Edgley, who informed him *that it was not Hallows's department to have received this money, and that he had no right whatever to have asked for it.*

The following sums are taken from Mr. Kay's books, as paid by him for the relief of Betty Al-len, a pauper of the township of Radcliffe.

	£	s	d	£	s	d
1789, October 30	3	0	0			
1790, July 30	1	16	0			
1791, June 30	3	6	0			
				8	2	0
	6	18	0			
1792, May 14	2	11	0			
October 30	1	16	0			
1793, April 30	1	19	0			
October 30	1	19	0			
1795,	3	4	6			
				12	7	6
				20	9	6

The

The receipt of 1789, is in Mr. Kay's book, as follows, "*paid to Manchester overseer,*" without signature, and appears like the hand-writing of Mr. Unite. The receipts of July 1790 and June 1791, are signed R. UNITT. I have not had an opportunity of examining whether the first sum is placed to the credit of the town, as those books are still in the possession of individuals not in office, instead of being kept in a proper place for the inspection of the public. The books for the years 1790 and 1791, I have carefully examined, but cannot find the sums received by Unite any where placed to the credit of the town.

The subsequent sums of money appear in Mr. Kay's books to have been paid to Mr. Edgley, by his receipts annexed to each payment; but in looking over Mr. Edgeley's account with the town, he appears to have debited himself with the receipt of only eighteen shillings, on the 14th of May 1792, instead of two pounds eleven shillings. The whole of the next payment is entered in his books, but as the payments of April and October 1793, are not to be found there, it is incumbent upon Mr. Edgley to shew to the public how he has accounted for these sums, as well as the last payment of three pounds four shillings and six-pence made to him in the present year, for to this period Betty Allen has been regularly paid *one shilling and six-pence per week out of the town's cash.*

These peculatory transactions have been greatly aided by Mr. Unite's departure from the plan adopted by Mr. Beaumont. Had he, on receiving the directions of Overseer Kay, to pay Betty Allen one shilling and six-pence per week, entered in her *pay ticket, on the cashier,* that she belonged to *Radcliffe parish,* she would not in that case have been considered as a *Manchester pauper,* nor would these gentlemen so long have escaped detection.

Though

Though Mr. Hallows does not appear to have received any part of this money, it is evident that he had received from Unite the necessary instructions, the circumstance of the letter which was " *written by his* CLERK," making a claim for *sixteen pounds two shillings,* is a convincing proof of his address. As the pupil and coadjutor of Unite, he seems to have made a tolerable proficiency in this sort of business; and had he been continued in office, bid fair to arrive at an equal degree of celebrity with his renowned tutor.

By the *pretended loss* of all the books, together with the letters from country overseers, necessary for an investigation of transactions of this nature, I am precluded from a possibility of ascertaining the amount of monies received, which I am well convinced is of sufficient magnitude to claim the immediate attention of the gentlemen now in office; and it is a duty incumbent on them to discover, if possible, how much Mr. Hallows has been involved in such like transactions, before they satisfy any claim which he may set up against the town.

It appears to me, that Mr. Unite has been, for some time, winding up the old concerns, without troubling his successors with the receipts of any arrears incurred in his overseership. He has very artfully taken care to leave no record behind, to trace his connections with country overseers, so that there is no mode of detection, but by examining the books of all the townships, not merely in this county, but throughout the kingdom, which would be attended with infinite trouble and expence, and which would not altogether, as appear by the following examinations, shew the extent of such like peculation. A snug agent, in a large town, has been found preferable to having transactions registered in parish books.

Birmingham.

Birmingham. The examination of Carolina Eyres, who says, that Jonathan Eyres, late of Manchester, was taken up with a warrant by Ralph Howard, for having left his wife chargeable to that township; that he was sentenced to six months imprisonment in the New Bayley; during which period he became so weak, that he was sent to the poorhouse, where in a few weeks he recovered, so as to enable him to assist in brewing and baking, for three or four months. Says, that he again left Manchester for Birmingham, and was again taken up by Ralph Howard, who confined him in prison until he entered into an agreement with Mr. Unite, to pay the money he owed to the town of Manchester, by instalments, to one Bramley, *a distant relation of Mr. Unite's,* who kept a toy-shop in Litchfield-street, Birmingham. At this time Mr. Unite received from this examinant three pounds fifteen shillings *for the expences of his journey, lock-up-house, and warrant.* That Jonathan Eyres paid Mr. Bramley *four shillings per week regularly for many months,* until Mr. Bramley told him that he had no occasion to call with it weekly, that he might pay it by larger instalments. Says, the three pounds fifteen shillings was paid by her to Mr. Unite, in the presence of Ralph Howard, and that she herself afterwards paid on account of Jonathan Eyres, to Mr. Bramley, the following sums of one pound, two pounds two shillings, eighteen shillings, one pound one shilling, and the last payment one pound eighteen shillings, amounting to seven pounds, *besides the weekly sums paid by Jonathan Eyres.* Says, *she always saw Mr. Bramley, or his daughter, enter each payment into a small book.* That Jonathan Eyres inlisted as a soldier, and when he left Birmingham, he was only indebted to the town of Manchester six weeks pay.

E   Signed

(26

Signed　CAROLINE EYRES.
Witness, RALPH HOWARD.
Birmingham, 28th Jan. 1794.

Examination of Ralph Howard, taken at Birmingham, who says, that he took up by order of Mr. Unite, *four run-away husbands,* two were acquitted by the magistrates at Manchester, one, Jonathan Eyres, was sentenced to six months imprisonment at Manchester. Says that the other, whose name he has forgot, *settled with Mr. Unite at Birmingham, and was discharged by Justice Carles, at Handsworth.* Says, he cannot say the amount of the money Unite received, but that he heard it was *considerably more than the sum which appeared* owing by Jonathan Eyres, and that *he gave Mr. Unite his note for the money, with security, and that two housekeepers were bound with him for the payment of it.* Says, that he made application to Mr. Bramley, who now keeps a public-house in the neighbourhood of Birmingham, to know the amount of the sums paid by Jonathan Eyres, but Bramley having mislaid the book, in which they were entered, promised to search for it, and inform him of the amount the next day. Mr. Bramley told Howard that any money paid on Eyre's account, might be paid him very safely. *That he very frequently received monies on such like occasions, for Mr. Unite, and which he was always punctual in remitting to him.*

Signed, RALPH HOWARD.

The above conversation between Mr. Bramley and Ralph Howard passed in my presence.

Cash said to be received by Mr. Unite, on Jonathan Eyre's account, at Birmingham and Manchester.

1791. Sept.

1791. Sept. 7. Cash paid Unite by J.
Eyres, at Manchester 2 12 6
Do. at Birmingham, by Car. Eyres........... 3 15 0
Do. Do. by instalments, *to Mr. Unite's
agent*.. 7 0 0
Do. weekly payments for several months,
not knowing the sum 0 0 0

13 7 6
By cash accounted for by Unite .. 2 12 0

Balance, for which there is no credit
given 10 15 6

To this sum the *note*, received by Unite at
Birmingham, which Howard believes from hearsay
to be about twenty pounds, should be added.

It should be observed that Mrs. Taylor, at the
workhouse, mentioned different sums owing at
Birmingham, for board at the Manchester workhouse, to Mr. Hallows, who was going there on
the town's business, *but on his return, he told Mrs.
Taylor, that he could not find them.*

Edward Rogers, a run-away husband, gave a
bond to Edward Hulme, a beadle of Manchester,
whilst he was in London, to indemnify this town
from the expence of maintaining his family, then
in the workhouse. Some time after Mr. Taylor,
as assistant to Mr. Unite, went to London on business for the town of Manchester, and called upon
Rogers, then in partnership with Mr. Baker, in an
extensive printing concern at Bow, in Essex, who
would have then paid him the money, which was
upwards of thirty pounds, but Mr. Taylor not being in the possession of the bond, he declined payment. Mr. Taylor, in consequence, called upon
Mr. Milne's agent, who advised him to write to
Manchester, and to stay in town until the return of
post,

post, when after waiting a week, he received Mr.
Unite's letter informing him that *the bond was lost!*
'. Mr. Taylor at the same time, by order of Mr.
Unite, called upon the Rev. Mr. ——, one of the
chaplains to the Prince of Wales, for money owing to the town of Manchester, for two bastard
children, registered in the *Red Basil Book,* but this
gentleman was from home at the time of Mr.
Taylor's application.

If any credit can be paid to Mr. Unite's story,
that 'Mr. Beaumont sent for him to Eccles, *to
tell him, when on his death-bed,* that *the Red Basil
Book was of no use,* for that all sums likely to be
received, were selected, and notes given for the
amount, it is evident Mr. Unite did not believe
him, otherwise he would not afterwards have made
such numerous applications for monies registered
in that book; but it plainly appears, that every
clue to the avenue of disclosure, is wanting; the
LETTER-BOOK, *with its corresponding letters,*
CASH-BOOK, VISITING-BOOK, BONDS,
CERTIFICATES, BASTARDY ORDERS,
*appear to be lost, or fraudulently withheld; in
fact, there is no record left that leads to the developement of these transactions.*

The following account of Mrs. Hallows, which,
with several of the preceding, stamps an indisputable
credit on the testimony of Mr. Taylor, relative to
Unite's private accounts, and the method of doing
business with country overseers. She says, that her
husband *received no books from Mr. Unite, when he
quitted the office, from which he could learn what
poor he was to relieve, and that he received only a
SINGLE SHEET OF PAPER, with the names of
ONE HUNDRED AND EIGHTEEN PAUP-
ERS, mentioning their places of abode, and the weekly payments, amounting to twelve pounds ten shillings.*

That

*That many paupers applied, whose names were not on
the paper, and Mr. Hallows refused to relieve them.
Says, that they then applied to Mr. Unite, and returned with notes from him that they were to receive
weekly pay. Says, that Mr. Hallows gave many paupers weekly relief, conceiving that they were* MANCHES-
TER POOR, but that he has since *discovered* MANY
OTHERS *who had weekly relief, that belonged to other
parishes,* and which have since *reimbursed the money
to this town.* One instance may be mentioned at
Wharton-in-the-Fyld, where *thirty pounds* have
lately been paid by the overseers of that township
to the overseers of Manchester, for money advanced out of the town's cash, for the relief of a
pauper, from April 1790 to December 1794, who
belonged to Wharton-in-the-Fyld, OF WHICH
THERE APPEARED NO ACCOUNT.

Mr. Unite in this transaction, was like Mr. Hallows at Radcliffe, who, by giving too long credit,
lost both principal and interest.

In Birmingham, the overseers' accounts are
kept with as much regularity as those of the first
commercial houses. *A statement of the parochial
accounts, from Easter to Easter, are laid before the
public,* to which is added a list of the present OUT
POOR, NURSE CHILDREN, FOREIGN RESIDENTS,
RUN-AWAY HUSBANDS, ARREARS IN BASTARDY,
with an explanation of the RECEIPTS and EXPEN-
DITURE OF THE TOWN.

The account given of their out poor, as published, is an exact copy of their visiting book,
which is kept in the following manner.

Names.	Age.	What Children.	Where they live.	Visitor's Report.

This

This register is regularly kept, and published annually, and I am informed it has been of great service in the detection of impostors. *In the preface of the visitor's report, at Birmingham, the inhabitants are recommended to peruse it with attention, and when it appears the public money is in any respect improperly applied, that information may be conveyed to the overseers, either personally, or by letter, when every attention will be paid, and secrecy observed, if required.*

It further proceeds, " *we observe too, with great concern, that the public bounty is much abused in the article of clothing given to the out poor, which expences have of late exceeded all former sums, and many abandoned wretches have been detected in pawning and selling the parish apparel. To prevent this shameful practice in future, it is proposed to deliver out clothes* AT HALF PRIME COST *to those who bring respectable recommendations.*"

Many respectable Ley-payers of this town have expressed a desire of having a yearly report, from our overseers, printed ; but this, for *weighty reasons*, has not been complied with. The abuses last year in the distribution of clothing, appear incredible, for many who enjoyed these donations, were undeserving. Clothing and goods have been indiscriminately given to almost every person who made application. There appears by the *overseers' tickets*, to have been near THREE THOU-SAND PAIR OF SHOES *given from the workhouse last year*, which far exceed the whole collective number of the preceding *seven years !*—It was then no uncommon thing for such people, who had received this charity, even in the severest part of the winter, to offer money in exchange at different shops for *slender shoes*, and very frequently for *stuff slippers*. It has likewise been the practice of giving from the workhouse

goods

goods *undyed,* that the poor might get them finished
to their own taste. *The workhouse colour* was so
generally known, that many of the poor would
not appear clothed with it. By thus distributing
goods in an unfinished state, the overseers have
very *skilfully* saved the expence of dying, and it
has given those who were desirous of pawning or
selling, advantage of the best market. It has likewise been observed, that different kinds of goods,
such as *clothing made up, shoes,* &c. &c. have been
retailed *new,* at little more than *half cost,* by deal-
ers in clothes, to whom the poor had disposed of
them.

According to Mrs. Hallows's account, various
people were improperly relieved in *Mr. Unite's* and
Mr. Edgley's time, as overseers. Says, one *Alice
Jowett* received three shillings per week from the
town, at a time when she was possessed of considerable property. That Mr. Hallows visited her
unknown, as overseer, when he found she had
purchased a house, for which she had paid one
hundred and sixty pounds. The numerous impo-
sitions of this sort, and monies otherways improperly applied, shew the necessity of a *regular visiting-book,* and *annual report.*

Mr. Wood, in his account of the Shrewsbury
House of Industry, says, " much unnecessary expence is unavoidably incurred, by committing the
relief and management of the poor to annual officers. They are obliged to relieve, because they
cannot employ. Unacquainted, likewise, with
their poor, when they enter on their offices, they
are the dupes of their frauds and artifice. And
when they begin to acquire a knowledge of their
characters and dispositions, they are superseded
by others, as destitute of this necessary information as they were themselves. It may appear a *bold,* but, perhaps, will not be found a
groundless

groundless assertion, that nearly one-half of the money expended on the parochial poor is misapplied, in consequence of the want of this acquaintance with, and experience of the artful stratagems they have recourse to, in order to extort undeserved relief." .

But to do away as much as possible this kind of imposition, I have recommended the methods made use of in many large towns, by advertising the names and residence of the poor, who receive weekly relief; and I am happy to find the gentlemen of No. 3 division, have adopted this plan, which cannot fail of having its desired effect. Many names will, in all probability, appear in the present quarterly accounts published, to be impostors, and others will become industrious, rather than have their names published as receiving parish relief *.

- The great regulations which have taken place at Shrewsbury, will be seen by the following account of the expences of the out-poor, including nurses' pay, &c. which have *annually* DECREASED as follows.

1784 to	1795	833	19	8
1785	1786	535	19	0
1786	1787	364	0	7
1787	1788	396	15	5
1788	1789	320	14	7½
1789	1790	322	17	5

The *sums* RECEIVED for support of *bastard children, certificate poor,* &c. have *annually* INCREASED as follows.

1784

---

* Since the publication of the above report, the overseers of No. 3 district have received information of several improper persons being relieved, which are struck off the list.

1784 to 1785 ········142 10 8
1785 ······1786 ········197 10 7
1786 ······1787 ········196 5 3
1787 ······1788 ········189 9 10
1788 ······1789 ········185 12 1
1789 ······1790 ········286 12 1

It appears from the statement, as per contra, that the expences of the out-poor have been regularly *decreasing* since the year 1785, from eight hundred and thirty-three pounds nineteen shillings and eight-pence, to three hundred and twenty-two pounds seventeen shillings and five-pence; and the *receipts* from other parishes for *certificated poor*, and *bastard children*, have *increased*, in six years, more than *double the amount!* But what a contrast do our accounts exhibit, when compared with theirs— instead of lessening our yearly expenditure, it has nearly increased to THREE TIMES *the sum ;* and our receipts in *certificate cases*, and *monies received from country overseers* have DECREASED, considerably *more than* ONE-HALF! If we are not entirely blinded by our prejudices, let us view the situation of other townships, contrasted with our own. At Shrewsbury, the reduction in the expence of supporting their poor, since the opening of the House of Industry, as stated in the last report of the directors, is SIXTEEN THOUSAND AND THREE POUNDS, exclusive of a balance of TWO THOUSAND FOUR HUNDRED POUNDS and upwards, in the treasurer's hands.

The following comparative statement of the house expences at Liverpool, in the years 1792 and 1793, with the two preceding years of 1790 and 1791, shews the necessity of a reformation in Manchester.

COMPARATIVE STATEMENT OF THE HOUSE EXPENCES AT LIVERPOOL.

1790.	£. s. d.	1791.	£. s. d.	Average. £. s. d.
Milk and Butter	935 13 8	Ditto	923 4 6	929 9 1
Coals	360 6 0	Ditto	374 7 6	367 6 9
Further expences	8726 14 4	Ditto	6801 18 10	9232 10 8¾
		Ditto of this year, paid off in 1792 }	2936 8 3½	

1792.	£. s. d.	1793.	£. s. d.	Average. £. s. d.	Less per Ann. £. s. d.
Milk and Butter	398 19 3	Ditto	479 9 11	439 4 7	490 4 6
Coals	213 9 7	Ditto	241 19 5¼	227 13 7¼	139 12 10¼
Further expences	5128 6 5½	Ditto	5878 18 10½	7014 5 2	2218 5 6½
Tradesmen paid in 1793 }	1491 18 0	Ditto unpaid	1530 0 0		

HOUSE EXPENCES LESSENED IN EACH YEAR £2848 2 11¼

	Tons.	C.	Q.	Lb.	Ton.	C.	Q.	Lb.
Beef used in the House from 6th June, 1789, to 5th June 1790, was	47	19	2	16				
Pork same time	4	10	2	3				
					52	10	0	19
Beef used from 25th March, 1791, to 25th March, 1792	29	0	1	6				
Salt Beef	1	0	0	0				
Pork ...... ditto	1	16	0	0				
					31	16	1	6
					20	13	3	13

BEEF AND PORK LESS USED IN ONE YEAR, TWENTY TON THIRTEEN HUN-DRED THREE QUARTERS AND THIRTEEN POUNDS! which *is a saving, at four-pence* per pound, of SEVEN HUNDRED AND SEVENTY-TWO POUNDS ELEVEN SHILLINGS!

It is curious to remark, that during the period in which this surprising *decrease* in the consumption of *butchers' meat* took place, there was an average *increase* of TWO HUNDRED AND SIX PAUPERS WITHIN, *and a still greater number* WITHOUT *doors, and all the poor were as well supplied with provisions, as in the preceding year!* And what is still more extraordinary, notwithstanding this *increase* in the poor, and the great advance in the price of *wheat, oatmeal,* and *potatoes,* added to the expence of erecting a *large range of buildings,* besides no sales whatever being made of spun cotton, yet the annual expences of the house were diminished more than TWO THOUSAND EIGHT HUNDRED POUNDS! and the funds of the year 1793, after an ample allowance for losses and errors, proved FIFTEEN HUNDRED POUNDS superior to the calculation *in favour of the town,* at the commencement of that year, and left a surplus of FOUR THOUSAND POUNDS! These beneficial effects may be justly attributed to the constant and judicious attention of the gentlemen who have so laudably exerted themselves to correct the parochial abuses of Liverpool. And I must not omit to do justice to the characters of Mr. Halliday the treasurer, and the overseers of that town, who favoured me with an inspection into their books, which exhibit a precedent highly worthy the imitation, not only of the overseers of Manchester, but of all the parish officers in the kingdom. Many other surrounding townships, notwithstanding the badness of the times, and the great price of provisions, have more or less *decreased their annual disbursements,* whilst a kind of party spirit in Manchester, continues an obstacle to the benefit which the public would derive from the regulations and instructions suggested by the Report of the Associated Ley-payers, and this is permitted

to

to exist, though the town is burthened with a debt of more than FOURTEEN THOUSAND POUNDS! besides the *annual* expenditure having increased, since the year 1790, from EIGHT THOUSAND to upwards of TWENTY THOUSAND POUNDS per annum!

The following accounts are selected from the printed Report of Birmingham, beginning with Easter 1786, in which I have made a comparative statement with those of Manchester.

From Easter 1786 to Easter 1787.

Composition money, (in Manchester termed "Hush money")	344	18	0			
Certificate cases REPAID by other parishes	325	3	10			
				670	1	10

Easter 1787 to Easter 1788.

Composition money, &c.	332	3	0			
Certificate cases	246	6	4			
				578	9	4
			£1248	11	2

The following is a MANCHESTER STATEMENT during the period of Mr. *Unite*'s overseership.

April 29th, 1790, to April 29th 1791.

Composition money, (WISELY termed " Hush money,") from *four gentlemen*	101	5	0
To cash from the overseers of other parishes for board of their poor in our workhouse, weekly payments by order of country overseers, certificate cases, and pensions, &c. &c. only said to be received this year	26	11	0
	127	16	0

:   Brought forward 127 16 0
From May 2d, 1791, to May 2d, 1792.
. *Composition, or "Hush money,"*
  from four gentlemen........117 10 0
To cash of country overseers,
    &c.* 31 2 0
                         148 12 0

                            £276 8 0

which makes a difference of the receipts in cash,
in "HUSH-MONEY," and CERTIFICATE CASES
alone, £972 3s.
It appears from the head overseer's books, that
there has only been received *twenty-nine pounds
eight shillings and six-pence* for. ALL *the boarders in
the Manchester workhouse* for TWO YEARS!
and in the above time there only appears credit
given for EIGHT SHILLINGS for ONE WOMAN
lying-in, and *one pound sixteen shillings for filiation
orders.* On the 4th, 15th, 19th, and 23d of June
1790, (*the time of Mr. Beaumont's indisposition*)
Mr. Unite appears regularly to have paid Mr.
Farrington for four filiation orders, at six shillings each; but, *after the death of Mr. Beaumont,*
which was on the 30th of the same month, Mr.
Unite does not appear to have accounted for a
single order, during the following ten months of
Mr. Farrington's churchwardenship. The next
that appears entered is the 19th of December
1791, after a lapse of eighteen months. *Another* entry is made of six shillings for one of
these orders on the 21st of January 1792; but
on the 16th of May following Mr. Unite has
accounted for *one hundred and eight* orders, a-
mounting to THIRTY-TWO POUNDS EIGHT SHIL-
LINGS! It should be noticed, that this money
                                     is

is received by *separate* payments, *casually* made, at six shillings each, during a period of more than TWO YEARS! For the appearance of this sum, I rather believe the town is indebted to Mr. Edgley, he having, in the absence of Mr. Unite, received one or both of the intermediate sums, which he took to Mr. Horsfall the treasurer; and on explaining to him the nature of these accounts, and the monies received, he declared it was the first cash he had ever received on the same occasion. On which Mr. Edgley observed with some surprize, that it was not the first by many that he OUGHT TO HAVE RECEIVED! This accounts in some measure, for the credit given for the sum of thirty-two pounds eight shillings, after more than a *two years* collection, in a GROSS SUM!

In my Reply to Mr. Unite, page 15 to 20, there is a complete jumble of accounts, or chapter of confusion, *collector, churchwarden, overseer,* &c. &c. *all* appear in the wrong. Mr. Edgley's disbursements, amounting to £2377 19*s.* 10½*d.* are cast up £2419. 6*s.* 5*d.* a difference in his favour of £41. 6*s.* 6½*d.* But this account, as well as the accounts of those higher in office, *may in all probability proceed from* MISTAKE, yet I am inclined to think, had this sum of £41. 6*s.* 6½*d.* been against Mr. Edgley, it would have stood a better chance of being found out at the close of the year, and not have been passed " ADJUSTED, EXAMINED," and ATTESTED UPON OATH!!

When *mistakes* are numerous, and ALL appear tending the same way, every unprejudiced reader must naturally think unfavourably.

In the bastardy account there appears to have been paid in *two years*, commencing April 1790, and ending May 2d, 1792............£2650.

And

Brought forward £ 2650.
And in the same period we appear
to have received *only*...................... 820.

Loss——£ 1320.

which is a difference of near *seventy per cent.*
while most of the large towns through the kingdom make this a profitable concern. In the Report published at STOCKPORT, June 1794, the
entries are as follow.

To cash received on bastardy account	85	7	4
By ditto paid on ditto...........................	77	4	3
PROFIT £	8	3	1

The above accounts shew a saving of more than
ten and a quarter per cent. whilst our *immaculate
overseers lose near seventy per cent.*

To what motives must the public attribute this
astonishing loss? for supposing the officers of
Stockport had transacted business to the extent of
that in Manchester, the *parish of Stockport* would
have gained ten and a quarter per cent. amounting
to more than TWO HUNDRED AND SEV-
ENTY-ONE POUNDS! which would have
been applied to the relief of the poor, IN RE-
DUCTION OF THE RATES TO BE LEVIED ON THE
INHABITANTS; but, by the management of the
overseers of Manchester, there is *a biennial loss* of
EIGHTEEN HUNDRED AND THIRTY
POUNDS! which occasions additional rates to be
levied on the inhabitants, by a comparative calculation of our *loss* and their *gain,* of more than TWO
THOUSAND GUINEAS. And it is still more
extraordinary that this difference should exist be-
tween *two manufacturing towns* not SEVEN MILES
DISTANT from each other.

Mr. Edgley, in March 1794, at the request of
the Associated Ley-payers, gave in an account of
the arrears in bastardy, which (exclusive of the

arrears

arrears contained in the *Red Basil Book)* amounted to twelve hundred and forty pounds, though this sum did not constitute the *whole* of the arrears subsequent to the dates of the said book. It likewise appears from the dates of the BASTARDY ORDERS, that a great part of these subsequent arrears *originated in Mr. Unite's overseership*, and though there is not a less number than TWO HUNDRED AND FORTY-SIX *defaulters*, yet, I do not find the amount of *five pounds accounted for by Mr. Unite during the whole course of his overseership.* There appear on the face of these accounts ma.iy people of property and credit, that are indebted very considerable sums, of several years standing, and who have not till within these few weeks been applied to. The very confused state of these accounts, and Mr. Hallows not having yet given up his books, prevent the present overseers from collecting these balances. They are, likewise, afraid of issuing warrants, lest the accounts should be found *settled and the monies not accounted for*, which would, in that case, subject them to an action for false imprisonment. We have a recent instance of this sort, where a *second warrant* was granted for arrears in bastardy, though security was lodged in the hands of the overseer for the payment of the *first*, the circumstance of no memorandum being made, nor credit given in the late overseers books, caused a journey *to Leeds*, where the mystery was unravelled.

In the accounts of bastardy, which constitute part of the above balance, *it appears that Mr. Unite has received different sums, which I cannot find credit given for.* Mrs. Hallows, likewise, gives an account of Mr. Unite being in possession of a note of hand, which appears in the list given in by Mr. Edgley, the balance whereof is twelve pounds two shillings. In the same book there appears an

G   account

account open since the year 1789, where no credit is given by Mr. Unite, though I am in possession of *many of his receipts, signed* R. UNITE,
given at the time he was OVERSEER, *and which he
continued to receive during his* CONSTABLESHIP, *to
a considerable amount !*

If epistolary evidence may be relied on, *Mr.
Hallows* has received many sums in bastardy, *as well
as on other accounts,* that he may, in all probability,
in the hurry of business, have omitted to enter. It
is, in my opinion, highly necessary, that these books
should undergo *an immediate inspection.* Surely
it is a time most fit to correct abuses of this nature, when the funds of the town are in such a situation as to have lost the confidence of every
tradesman who has served the house ; and, if I
am not misinformed, the poor might now starve
for want of necessaries, were they not supported
by the *personal* credit of the present overseers.

It has been from time immemorial the constant
practice of overseers, to enter all paupers received
into the workhouse, as boarders, *(when they were
not to be supported at the expence of the town) in the
governor's book,* as a *reduction* of the house expences ; but this practice *(for reasons too obvious
to need a comment)* WAS TOTALLY DISCONTINUED
BY MR. UNITE !

Mrs. Taylor gives an account of one John
Shannon, who was sent into the house by Mr.
Unite, the 1st of December 1790, *without Mr.
Unite ever mentioning that he belonged to a sick club,*
which was held at Ellis Rose's, the Dyers-arms, in
Long-mill-gate. On the 14th of the same month,
the stewards of the club came to the workhouse,
and paid John Shannon twelve shillings, being two
weeks allowance, and on the 21st of the same
month, the stewards brought six shillings more,
which Mrs. Taylor, the governess, took from him,

John

John Shannon, on account of his incapacity to take care of it. On the same, or following, day, Mr. Unite came to the workhouse, and demanded of Mrs. Taylor the money she had received of Shannon, saying, *that he had* PAID *his quarterage into the box,* and therefore *he would receive* HIS PAY. Mrs. Taylor told Mr. Unite, that he was *mistaken about his paying the money into the box for Shannon, as it was the general method of the stewards to deduct the quarterage from their pay.* The whole sum really paid amounted to six pounds and three-pence, to the 20th of April, when Shannon died. Though Mr. Unite received these sums *weekly,* save one payment of twelve shillings for a fortnight's pay, there appears only a credit given for five pounds nine shillings, which *is on the 14th. of April* entered in GROSS!

The society of *Fustian-cutters,* in the time of Mr. Unite's overseership, had to find a substitute to serve in the militia, for one of their members who was ballotted, which they procured and paid for out of the box; and Mr. Unite *received for this society the usual allowance of four guineas: repeated* applications have since been made from the society to recover this money, but to no effect. Mr. Unite avails himself *of the old excuse, that the town is indebted to him such large sums of money, as to prevent him from paying his private credit.* I shall not be presumptuous enough to say, that this *hackneyed story* is told to tradesmen, his creditors, as a subterfuge to avoid the payment of his debts; but certainly it appears that his salary has been paid him quarterly, and that he has always been in possession of monies for the use of the town.

In the *orders of filiation* made by the magistrates, for the maintenance of bastard children, a sum of money is usually allowed for the expences

of

of lying-in, exclusive of the weekly allowance for the support of *these women. at the work-house; but this practice was discontinued by Mr. Unite, who, during the time of his overseership, sent a great number of women to lie-in, and kept them very often many months after their delivery, at the expence of the town, without paying the governor any thing under the order.*

One CHRISTIANA GASKILL lay-in. at the workhouse twice, and continued there with *her children* considerably more than twelve months, whilst the fathers of both children made regular payments, and for several years after, agreeably to the orders. Upon her delivery of the latter child, one pound eighteen shillings were paid for lying-in, which should have appeared to the credit of the town, for the indulgence of the workhouse, yet, there only appears accounted for, in the whole, three pounds five shillings received from both fathers.

Mrs. TAYLOR, the governess of the work-house, says, that she has spoken of Mr. Unite's conduct to Mr. Horsfall, and of his receiving these monies; and that she told him, if an overseer was allowed to *board* people in the workhouse, and to proceed as Mr. Unite had done, it *would be adviseable to put up the overseership by auction, and sell it to the best bidder!*
Mr. HORSFALL required Mrs. Taylor to make out a list of such people who had had the indulgence of the workhouse in Unite's time, which was made out accordingly, amounting to between sixty and seventy pounds.—Says, that Mr. Horsfall told the governor, that he thought Mr. Unite had accounted for *some part of it.*

Mrs.

Mrs. Taylor further says, that it was *very often* the case, when poor women came to receive their, weekly pay under the order of the magistrate, for the support of their children, *to complain of Mr. Unite having withheld their filiation orders*, AND KEPT PART OF THEIR PAY!

Says, that she gave from the workhouse *great quantities of wearing-apparel*, by ORDER of Mr. Unite, *to the poor of other parishes, and which Mr. Unite always took an account of.* That she gave one Mary Fazakerly, *who belonged* to Liverpool, in the month of December 1791, the following wearing-apparel, viz.

	s.	d.			
Two pairs of shoes....7	4				
Two bed-gowns 4	6				
Six yards of linen....4	4½				
Six yards blue plain 7	9	£.	s.	d.	
		1	4	1¼	

Mr. Unite got the above account made out, and TOOK HER HIMSELF *the following morning to Liverpool.* The above curious account of clothing given, with *linen* UNMADE, to a woman who was immediately removed to her place of settlement, I do confess, has a strange appearance; but, far be it from me even to insinuate any incontinent remark here—yet, for the reputation of Mr. Unite, I sincerely wish that * he had not forgotten to bring back with him the *one pound four shillings.*

Mrs. Taylor gives an account of Ann Chadwick, who lay-in of twins in the workhouse, in April 1792, where she continued a month, when two men from Timperley, in Cheshire, took her away, and paid Mr. Unite £1 5s.—Says, by order of Mr. Unite, she provided one Linney's children, belonging to Newton, with wearing apparel, amounting to one pound twelve shillings and ten-pence.

That

That one ROBERTS, a pauper belonging to Chorlton, was supported in the workhouse, and that the overseers of Chorlton were to pay, *two shillings per week* for his maintenance. That after the death of Mr. Beaumont he continued in the workhouse forty-eight weeks, when he died.—Says, that to her knowledge, fifteen shillings were paid Mr. Unite, December 16, 1791, for Ann Travis, and child, for board.—That one George Griffith paid for Hellen Folkes's lying-in, March 8, 1792, one pound one shilling.—That Mary Horton, of Ashton, was only in the house one week, when Mr. Unite insisted on the overseer paying for that time five shillings, which was paid in her presence.

It appears, likewise, from the head church-warden's cash-book, in 1791, that Mr. Beaumont's executor was paid *four pounds sixteen shillings* for goods for Mr. Unite; and that he, Mr. Unite, had from the poor-house, a quantity of *sheets, blankets, rugs,* and *towelling,* that does not appear to his debit. The balance, likewise, due to the town from Mr. Unite, of *seventeen pounds,* since April 1793, I do not find accounted for.

CHARLES MOLLINEAUX *and his wife,* in Hilton's-entry, Fennel-street, were taken into the workhouse in the month of November 1790. He was to pay three shillings per week for his board, and the service of his wife was to be considered equal to the expences of her support. On the 25th of July 1791, Mollineaux paid Mr. Unite four pounds fourteen shillings on this account, and three shillings the week following; that on the 11th of November he paid *Mrs. Unite* two pounds twelve shillings and six-pence; but says, that afterwards hearing that Mr. Unite was leaving the office of overseer, he asked him for a receipt, when Mr. Unite told him " *there was no fear, the*
money

money was down in Mr. Horsfall's books.". Mr. Hallows, who was to succeed Mr. Unite, was present at this conversation, and also said, that he had no occasion to be afraid. A copy of Mr. Horsfall's books and papers I have examined, where there appears a credit given for four pounds ten shillings, instead of *four guineas and a half,* the old method *five per cent. commission.* It is worthy of remark, that this money is stated to have been received on the 28th of June 1791, for thirty weeks; when the *real fact* appears to be, that the four pounds fourteen shillings and six-pence were not paid till the 26th of July 1791. *Nor is there any account given of the* TWO GUINEAS AND A HALF *paid to* MRS. UNITE. After this period Mr. Taylor had Mr. Horsfall's orders to receive the monies himself, which appear accounted for by Mr. Taylor till he left the house on Shrove Tuesday 1791.

It appears, likewise, from Mrs. Taylor's book, that Mr. Unite received the following sums from a Mr. Bracewell, for the board of Joseph Rider.

	£.	s.	d.
Cash received by Mr. Unite	4	10	0
1791, July 27th, Do.	3	3	0
Nov. 22, Do.	3	10	0
1792, Feb. 1, Do.	3	3	0
	£14	6	0
1791, Nov. 26, by cash accounted for by Mr. Unite	3	10	0
Balance, which Mr. Unite does not appear to have accounted for	£10	16	0

After the payment of the above sums, Mr. Taylor,

lor, the governor, received the remainder from Mr. Bracewell, amounting to seventeen pounds six shillings and six-pence, which the town has credit for.

A GENTLEMAN, in the neighbourhood of Piccadilly, paid, at two separate times, about thirty shillings, and which he was distrustful Mr. Unite had no right to have asked for; this also I cannot find accounted for.

Mrs. Taylor likewise observes, that during the time of Mr. Beaumont's overseership, she received at the workhouse considerable quantities of *household goods and wearing apparel; that it was then in her power to have stocked a poor family with almost every thing necessary, but, that since Mr. Unite came into office, neither goods, nor clothes, have ever found their way into the workhouse,* nor is the cash arising from the sales accounted for.

THOMAS DAVIS, constable, of Stretford, brought at different times to town in his cart, a great number of vagrants, the expences of which he ought to have been paid on delivery.

At one time he was desired by Mr. Unite *to leave his papers* which he did. That he afterwards called frequently, but that Mr. Unite always put him off, by pretending to be in a hurry, or some such frivolous excuse. That he sometimes saw *Mrs. Unite,* who appeared offended at his calling. The last time he called, he saw Mr. Unite, and told him he had had a great deal of trouble about his money, when Mr. Unite gave him to understand, that *the papers* he should have received his money from, were *lost!* This settled the business at once, and the constable *lost* his money.

The various instances of peculation are so numerous,

merous, that I shall only recite two or three of the following cases, merely to convince the reader, that they are of that complexion which could not have proceeded from mistake.

A YOUNG WOMAN in Fennel-street was delivered of a bastard child in the workouse, in the year 1789, and an order was made upon the father by the magistrates, to pay two guineas for her lying-in, and one shilling and nine-pence per week towards the maintenance of the child. The mother continued in the workhouse about one year and a half, during which time, and about *twelve months afterwards, she received no pay under the order.* At the expiration of this period, she began to receive weekly pay for about two years and a half, when Mr. Edgley found *Mr. Unite had been regularly receiving pay from the child's father during this time, though he* (Mr. Edgley) *had been paying her, out of the town's cash!* Mr. Edgley then informed her, that as Mr. Unite had regularly received the money from the child's father, she must apply to him for it. She accordingly waited on Mr. Unite, who told her, *that the town owed him so much money, that he could not then pay her.* She frequently repeated her applications, when the same answers were given, and she remained *six months* without pay. About eighteen months ago, this poor woman, by desire of Mr. Edgley, went into the country to enquire after the child's father, as it was Mr. Edgley's intention to serve him with a warrant for the money owing. On her return, she informed Mr. Edgley that he was at home, when Mr. Edgley gave her half a guinea, and observed, that *he had been with Mr. Unite the night before, who had acknowledged the receipt of the monies from the father of the child.* Mr. Edgley then desired her to attend on the next

H

nurses'

nurses' day, when he promised to pay her two guineas. Mr. Edgley from this time renewed her former allowance of one shilling and nine-pence per week, and continued it for about six months, when he again told her, that he was obliged to discontinue it, as he could not get the money which had been received by Mr. Unite. Says, she often afterwards made application to Mr. Edgley, who told her he would pay her no more, until he got the money from Mr. Unite, which, he said, amounted to between nine and ten pounds. She then applied to Mr. Unite, and took a shop-keeper with her from Newton-lane, who told Mr. Unite, that he had assisted her with provisions for a considerable time, or she would have perished for want, in consequence of which she owed him near forty shillings.—Mr. Unite again put her off, by telling her he was going to Lancaster assizes, and that he should receive a considerable sum, and would then pay her. She applied on the Saturday following, when Mr. Unite gave her two guineas; since which time she has received no pay whatever.

The following are payments made by Robert Allen, the father of the child, to Mr. Unite, as per his receipts.

1791, Aug. 9, received from
Allen 2 2 0
No date, do. 2 2 0
1792, Feb. 23d, do............. 1 11 6
April 26th, do............. 1 11 6
Ang. 25th, do............. 1 11 6
—————
8 18 6

The above receipts, to the 25th of August, are the hand-writing of MR. UNITE, though signed R. UNITT, as OVERSEER. On the same day, in another receipt, he signs UNITE as CONSTABLE, which

which is somewhat applicable, after the *union* of the *two offices;* but, had he signed his name CIPHER, and accounted for the cash he had received, I should have been half inclined to think he had both done justice to himself, and to the public.

It is worthy of remark, after the last payment on the 25th of August 1792, MR. UNITE observed to *Allen,* that he had only ONE more payment to bring him, *as it would then make up his books!* It appears that the late Mr. Beaumont received two pounds two shillings for Betty Allen's lying-in; but her board during eighteen months that she was in the workhouse, amounting to six pounds six shillings, and the different sums, as per Mr. UNITE's receipts, I do not find placed to the credit of the town.

It ought to be remarked that Mr. Edgley, paying Betty Allen out of the town's purse, *two years and a half,* without ever looking after the father of the child, is an unpardonable neglect. This poor woman I saw at the time she was deprived of her pay, in a very wretched and helpless situation; the small allowance, on which her existence, *and that of an* HELPLESS INFANT *depended, was withheld* and *pocketed* by an *unfeeling overseer.*

The following is another case, which differs from the last recited examination, and will be a further proof of peculation in bastardy.

A YOUNG WOMAN, in *Thomas's-street,* was delivered of a bastard child, on the 9th day of July 1788, which she afterwards fathered upon a weaver, before two magistrates, who made an order for lying-in, and a further sum of fourteen-pence per week towards the maintenance of the child. The young woman not having yet received her lying-in money, or any part of her weekly pay, a distant relation of hers, who had chiefly supported her,

repeatedly

repeatedly applied to Mr. Unite for the money, who always made some excuse of being engaged, and desired him to call again. At one of these applications, he was desired by Mr. Unite to stay, and he would pay him. This promise induced him to wait *nearly five hours*, during which period he repeatedly desired Mr. Unite to come to some settlement, as he had that night to go nine miles home. Mr. Unite then replied, *I have received about five pounds*, which is worth staying for. He therefore waited till he was deprived of all hopes of receiving the money, and at last came away without it. *Repeated applications were afterwards made to Mr. Unite, without effect.* On the 4th day of last December, he called upon Mr. Edgley, who told him *that he had never received any thing under the order*, to which he referred, and calculated the arrears due to twenty pounds six shillings, which Mr. Edgley observed, was a serious sum, but that he could render him no assistance, as *Mr. Unite had received the money.* This poor woman has never yet received *any thing* towards the expence of *lying-in, nor any thing towards the maintenance of her child, nor, has he ever given the town credit for the five pounds which he acknowledged to have received.*

On the *examination* of Mr. RALPH WILCOX-ON, it appears, that about fifteen months ago, his shop, in Smythy-door, was broke open, and property stolen to the amount of sixty pounds and upwards. The thieves were afterwards *taken, tried,* and *convicted.* That thirty-eight guineas in cash were found upon one of them. The magistrates, after the trial, ordered Mr. Unite to return to the prosecutor his money. Mr. Unite gave Mr. Wilcoxon, in a few days afterwards, twenty-eight guineas *only,* with this observation, " *I have made use*

of

of ten guineas, *do not mention it to any body, but call on me in the course of a fortnight, and I will pay you.*" Mr. Wilcoxon called according to Mr. Unite's appointment, who then said, " *I am not ready for you, call again.*" About a month afterwards the application was repeated, and the same answer given by Mr. Unite, with this further observation, *that he thought he should then keep the money, as they* (meaning the persons who were in prison under sentence of transportation) *had threatened him with law.* Mr. Unite, after some conversation with Mr. Wilcoxon, desired him to call again, and if *they* did not proceed by law, he should pay him the money. In a short time afterwards the prosecutor paid Mr. Unite another visit, who accosted him with these words, " *you scoundrel, how dare you open my door without knocking?*" The prosecutor stated the reason of his application, when Mr. Unite observed, that he should not pay him, *for that he could keep the money four years in his hands.* Mr. Unite then *ordered one of the beadles,* Jonathan Butterworth, *to take him immediately to the New Bayley, but the beadle only so far obeyed his direction, as to lay hold of him by the collar, and to turn him out of the yard.* The prosecutor having been thus insulted, has since discontinued his application, and Mr. Unite still keeps possession of his property.

About three months ago, Wilcoxon's wife applied, and painted the distress they were in, in consequence of being robbed, and having part of the goods to pay for, also a family of small children. Mr. Unite violently threatened, if she did not leave the door, he would have her confined in the New Bayley.

After Mr. Wilcoxon had lost his property, added to the expence of pursuing the thieves, Mr. Unite withheld from him, besides the ten guineas, two pairs of

silk and cotton stockings, which he told the prosecutor, though the stockings belonged to him, he had
no right to receive them, not having sworn there-
to, that they in that case belonged to the PO-
LICE OFFICE. Says, that Mr. Unite took a
fancy at that time to the pattern of a kerseymere
waistcoat piece, which the prosecutor gave him.

Mr. Unite, on examining the house of a Mr. Foreman, of Liverpool, who Mr. Unite had had information of his having bought part of these goods, seized and brought off with him a *quantity of shoes, waistcoat pieces,* and *gown pieces,* which Mr. Foreman has
not yet received back, nor do I find them any
where accounted for.

WILLIAM DARBYSHIRE, of *Manchester,*
callender-man, says, that several months ago he met
with Mr. Wilcoxon, at the Coach and Horses, in
Dean's-gate, who told him that Mr. Unite had to
pay him ten guineas, which he had kept out of
thirty-eight guineas, which the magistrates at the
New Bayley had ordered him to return. That he
had called very often, but could not get it from him.
This examinant promised to accompany him to Mr.
Unite's, but on Mr. Wilcoxon's opening his *back
door,* Mr. Unite immediately fell into a violent
passion, and called him a scoundrel, and asked
him how he durst presume to open his door without knocking. He then ordered Jonathan, the
beadle, to take Mr. Wilcoxon immediately to the
New Bayley. That on collaring Mr. Wilcoxon,
Mr. Unite stamped, and was so very outrageous,
that he, Darbyshire, was glad to get away.

SAMUEL DICKINSON, of *Long-mill-gate,*
Manchester, print-glazer, had in the month of January 1794, his warehouse broken open, and *several
pieces of printed calicoes and two glazing rollers*
stolen.

stolen. The thieves were afterwards taken, and convicted at the Manchester quarter sessions. After the trial he had an order to receive the goods back, as he had been at more than twenty pounds expence in apprehending them. Says, he made many applications to Mr. Unite, but could never receive any thing back from him, except the coarse calicoes. That there were about fifteen yards of fine chints, and two glazing rollers, which Mr. Unite kept. Says, that he applied many times for the *rollers* and the *chints*, At one of these applications, he saw *the rollers in Mr. Unite's house.* Says, that the goods stolen belonged to Mr. Greenways, and that they only charged him for the chints twenty-one pence per yard, in consideration of the loss he sustained, but, that they were the same as they sold at two shillings and four-pence. Says, that he called upon Mr. Unite very often, to get them back. That the last time but one he called, Mr. Unite told him *that his wife, or servants, had made them into rubbing rags.*

Dickinson, it should be observed, is a poor, industrious man, with a wife and several small children ; that the property stolen from his workshop, belonged to different masters ; that the loss he sustained, with the expence of making the search after these thieves, *detecting* and *bringing* them *to justice,* so much distressed him, that he was obliged, for the support of his family, to sell nearly all his furniture, and the only bed which he had to lie upon.

Mr. BENJAMIN MARLOW, *hatter,* and *special constable,* near Miles Platting, Newton-lane, was, about eighteen months ago, in the possession of a quantity of fustian, which Mr. Unite obtained from him on the plea that he suspected it to be stolen. About three months after, Mr. Unite finding his

suspicions

suspicions to be groundless, informed Mr. Marlow by one of the beadles, that he would send it him immediately. Some time after Mr. Marlow met by chance with Mr. Unite at *Peter Fearnhead's*, in Smithy-door, and asked him why he did not return him the fustian, when Mr. Unite replied, " I HAVE SOLD IT, AND GIVEN THE MONEY TO THE POOR," and immediately shut the door in his face. Mr. Marlow says, he stated to the company, "*that if the taking of his fustian, and never returning it, was law, there was no justice in the country.*"

, Mr. BENJAMIN WALKER, *innkeeper,* St. *Mary's-gate,* was robbed of *fifty guineas,* and a *silver watch,* in the month of December 1793, and also of *thirteen pounds five shillings,* the property of a sick club society, held in his house. The thief was afterwards apprehended in one of the duke's boats, by a Mr. Kay, with nearly the whole of the property upon him, including that which belonged to the sick club, and which he gave to Mr. Unite. The trial and conviction took place at the last March assizes; when Mr. Unite gave evidence that he had received upwards of sixty-four pounds of the property stolen. Immediately after the trial, Mr. Walker, the prosecutor, observed to Mr. Unite, that he would apply to the Judge that his property might be restored. Mr. Unite made answer, that was unnecessary, for that he would return it immediately on going out of court. The prosecutor made several applications in the course of the same day, but received only *evasive answers.* He then threatened to apply to the Judge the next morning, if his property was not returned to him, when Mr. Unite told the prosecutor, *he was very insolent.* On which Mr. Walker applied to Mr. Milne, the attorney for the prosecution, informing him, that he could not get his property

of

of Mr. Unite, that he was very hardly treated, and if Mr. Milne would make out his account, he would pay him immediately. On which Mr. Milne gave the prosecutor a note to Mr. Unite to deliver thirty guineas and his watch, which he received. Mr. Walker has since frequently applied to Mr. Milne for his bill, who always said he was busy. Says, that about a month after Mr. Battye's advertisement appeared in the Chester paper; he again applied to Mr. Milne, who again said, he had not time to make it out, That about four months ago, he desired Mr. Milne to get from Mr. Unite the remainder of the money, and let the business be settled, when Mr. Milne informed him, *that he would have nothing to do with Mr. Unite,* and that he should look upon him, Mr. Walker, for the payment of what was due to him. Mr. Walker appears to have been very desirous of paying Mr. Milne, whenever he could have got his bill; and till this period he was of opinion Mr. Unite, by Mr. Milne's order, kept this money as a guarantee for the payment of the bill. In consequence of Mr. Milne's information, he again applied to Mr. Unite, when he promised to call upon him and pay him the remainder of the money the day following, but Mr. Unite did not keep his promise. Mr. Walker, on the 10th of December last, met Mr. Unite in St. Ann's-square, when he again promised to call the next day, but Mr. Unite again broke his word, and still continues to withhold the remainder of Mr. Walker's money, *nineteen pounds* and upwards.

Examination of JOHN HARRISON, clerk of the collegiate church, Manchester, who says, "that he was a special constable, and that about Christmas 1792, one John Evans, of Balloon-street, found a box

box

box of cards about eight o'clock in the evening. That the box was so heavy, that it required two men to lift it, being about *four feet in length, two in breadth, and about two feet in depth.* Says, on Evans applying to him, this examinant, they went to Mr. Unite, as they suspected the goods were stolen. Mr. Unite ordered the cards to be taken to his house, which was done according to his directions, by Evans, in a wheelbarrow. Says, on Sunday the 30th of last November, he met with Mr. Unite by chance, at Mr. Matthew Green's, the Blackmore's-head, in Old-church-yard: that in the course of conversation, Mr. Unite said, *he supposed this examinant had something to charge him with,* who told him he had, and immediately declared the subject, and asked Mr. Unite, to defend himself. Mr. Unite replied, I have given the cards to the owner in the presence of the magistrates. This examinant then asked him, who the owner was. Mr. Unite said, he did not know the person's name, but he could find proof of its delivery. This examinant then said, it was very hard the poor man, who found the cards, and had so much trouble of taking so heavy a box to his house, should not have been rewarded in the course of *two years.* On which Mr. Unite said " *he had* LIBERALLY REWARDED *him,*" *and offered to lay this examinant a wager upon it.*

JOHN EVANS, of Balloon-street, sand-carrier, says, that in Christmas holidays 1792, he found a box of cards for carding cotton, in Hanover-street. That he applied to Mr. Harrison, the clerk of the Old-church, who went with him to Mr. Unite's house. Says, Mr. Unite desired the box to be brought to his office, and this examinant says he took it there in a wheelbarrow, and that it was so heavy that it required two men to put it in the barrow.

barrow. Says, Mr. Unite then ordered him to call again, and he would *advertise it ;*—he called on Mr. Unite the next morning, who told him, he could say nothing to him until it was advertised, and owned, when that was done, he should receive something *worth his while* for finding and bringing it.—Says, he saw Mr. Unite some time afterwards, who told him, he had not found the owner ;—nor could he learn from any other person, that it ever had been *advertised.* Says, that he saw Mr. Unite about a month before Whitsuntide, and he again told him, he had not yet found the owner.—Says, he again applied to Mr. Unite a *few days* before Whit Sunday, who told him then *he had* found the owner, and that he should have a handsome present, and desired he would call about the middle of Whitsun week. That he accordingly called in Whitsun week, when Mr. Unite told him, *that the owner had made him no present for finding it, or, he would have given him something.* Says, he called on Mr. Unite several times, who always told him, he had no money in his pocket, or he would have given him a SHILLING, but has never yet received any thing.

MARY CLAYTON, lived in service with Mr. KNOTT, *inn-keeper,* at *Ashton-under-line* and *Manchester,* near *thirteen years.* Says, she was pregnant, and within six weeks of her time, by a person of the name of Schneider, a musician in the first regiment of dragoons, and that Mr. Knott, her master, directed her to go to Mr. Unite, the overseer, and father her child. That she went according to his directions, to Mr. Unite, in Dolefield, who ordered her to call again ; that she again waited on Mr. Unite, who told her, that she had no right at that time to father her child, as he said, *there was a fresh act just new come up, against women*

women fathering their children until they had laid-in a month. Says, she told Mr. Unite, the regiment would leave the town before she should be brought to bed, and that he *(Schneider)* was not a *private soldier;—*that he had, besides his *billet, twelve shillings per week* from the regiment, and, *fifteen shillings per week* from Messrs. *Handy and Franklin,* with the money he got, by *teaching music.* Says, after having lain-in a month, she went before Justice Griffith, and there saw Mr. Hallows, (Mr. Unite having left the office of overseer) when her examination was taken on oath, but does not recollect what the magistrate's order specified, as Mr. Hallows kept it; to whom, she afterwards frequently applied for relief, but was always refused. That she had then no employment but that of washing for hire, and having to pay *four shillings per week* with her child at nurse, and *one shilling per week for a furnished room,* the little money she had saved in her servitude was exhausted, and she was obliged, in order to support herself and child, to sell her clothes. Says, she afterwards called on Mr. Hallows, who again refused her relief, and that she became so *enfeebled* and *sickly for want of food,* that she was taken to the Infirmary, where she continued *seventeen weeks.* That during her confinement, she requested a Mrs. Rayney, a shopkeeper in Cock-gates, to apply to Mr. Hallows, and explain to him the situation she was in in the Infirmary, and that the nurse had refused to keep her child any longer.—Says, application was made by a Mrs. Rayney, but to no purpose, as Mr. Hallows still refused to relieve her. At this time, the remaining part of her clothes were *pawned* and *sold* to pay the nurse. That when she got a little strength, she came out of the Infirmary, and had she not been relieved by different people in Cock-gates, with broken meat, &c. both herself and child must have perished for want.

Says, that she afterwards applied to Mr. *Wright*, grocer, in *Hanging-ditch*, who has since relieved her with one shilling per week.

MARTHA WESTLEY, *No.* 74, *Portland street*, wife of James Westley, now in the marine service, on board the Crescent frigate, who inlisted in one of the independant companies, in the year 1789, being anxious to regain the comfort and society of her husband, about three weeks before the Christmas following, she was induced to pledge *one silk gown, one printed gown, one black gown, one green quilted petticoat, one pair of stays, two white aprons, three silk handkerchiefs, two fine shifts, twelve pairs of cotton stockings, and other wearing-apparel, and, also one pair of sheets, for seven guineas*, which she sent to Chatham, in order to purchase her husband's discharge. That on his return through London, he went on board the Crescent frigate. That when her husband left her, she *had one child, and was big of another;*—that she belonged to Manchester, and being unable to support herself, she went to the workhouse, 6th of January 1790, and was brought to bed the Saturday following. That some time after her delivery, she was seized with a fever, and continued ill many weeks;—but on her recovery, so as to be capable of being led to Mr. Unite's house, in Dole-field, she proposed to give him the duplicates of her pledges, if he would release, and give her part of her clothes, that he might have the remainder, and she would go home to her friends at *Prees*, in *Shropshire*, and give the town no further trouble. Says, that Mr. Unite paid the waggoner, for her conveyance, and likewise *gave her a note to inform the overseer at Prees, that she belonged to Manchester.*

Mr.

Mr. Unite kept her pledges, and assured her, that she should have all her clothes, and that he would send them after her, and, if she could not support herself, *he would allow her two shillings per week, and that it should be paid weekly, monthly, or quarterly,* but when she got home, her father was so much dissatisfied at having to support her and her *two children,* that she wrote to Mr. Unite, *four letters, to get the allowance which he* promised her, but never yet was fortunate enough to receive an answer. That she was so infirm, that she could not come to Manchester, and therefore sent her sister to apply to Mr. Unite for her relief; but on application to Mr. Unite, as overseer, he refused to allow her any thing. That about two months after she came to Manchester herself, and frequently applied to Mr. Unite, but could not settle with him. He then gave her a note to go into the poor-house that night, and promised to settle with her the next day. That she went the next day, and the day following, to get the duplicates, and an allowance out of the poor-house. Mr. Unite then promised, if she would call *again,* he would then settle with her. Says, she continued in the workhouse TEN MONTHS, and during that time kept repeating her applications, but that she always received the same evasive answers, until she was tired of asking. Says, she lost the use of her limbs in the workhouse, and was taken in a carrying-chair to the Infirmary. That after she got better, and left the Infirmary, she applied to Mr. Hallows for a bed and bedding, which he gave her, and insisted on her getting the duplicates from Mr. Unite, and giving them to him. That she applied to Mr. Unite, who told her to give his *compliments* to Mr. Hallows, and tell him, that he had something else to do than to hunt for tickets for either her, or him. That Mr. Unite was in
such

such a passion, that she durst not apply again, and that she has never since received the tickets from him.

The *examination* of BETTY PIKE, taken at the Manchester workhouse, who says, that her husband was a miller, at Knott-mill, and rented a house of Mr. Gilbert, of Worsley, where they lived *two years*. That about fourteen weeks ago, (the beginning of October 1794) her husband left her with three children, the eldest under *five*, the second under *three*, and the youngest under *two* years of age. That her children and herself were nearly starved for want of food, having sold the chief part of her goods for their support. That she then applied for relief to Mr. Hallows, but, not knowing the place of her settlement, her application was fruitless. Further says, that she made application time after time, for more than a fortnight, without effect. That she afterwards applied at the New Bayley, but Mr. Hallows prevented her from appearing before the magistrates, by telling her, she must call upon him at his house. That she at this time begged him to have compassion on her children, who were ready to drop for want. Says, that she told Mr. Hallows she had a certificate at Baslow, in Derbyshire, and she then gave him directions to write, but that he again refused to relieve her; that she waited for some time with her children in such distress, that she was fearful they would have died of hunger;—no letter appearing, and it being then Saturday, Mr. Hallows promised if she would call on Monday, he would give her a pass, but again put her off without relief. On the following Monday she again applied, and saw *Mrs. Hallows*, who after some conversation, gave her a pass, and ordered her, before she arrived at Baslow, *to*

destroy

destroy it, to tear it in pieces, and not to let any body
look at it in Baslow. Further says, that Mr. Hallows gave her a ticket to get a pair of shoes at the
workhouse. That she set off with *a walking pass,*
with her children, in a very weak state *(having the*
fever, which was then so prevalent amongst the poor),
and on her arrival at Stockport, she made application to one Stopford, a constable; who examined
her respecting her removal, when she told him she
did not know where she belonged to, but that she
was going to enquire at Baslow for her certificate.
The constable took her before Mr. Prescot, the
rector, and a magistrate; and shewed him the pass..
That Mr. Prescot asked, who gave her the pass?
She replied, Mrs. Hallows. — He then asked
her, if she did not, on receiving the pass, go to
Mr. Griffith, the magistrate, to get it signed.
She told the rector, she did not, that Mrs. Hallows wrote it herself. On which the rector said,
it was not a right pass, that Mrs. Hallows had
done so frequently, and that she should proceed
no further with it; betwixt eleven and twelve
o'clock on the same day, she was ordered to meet
the magistrates, when Mr. Prescott observed,
that *Mrs. Hallows* acted *in Manchester both* as
overseer and justice; but added, the pass *might*
have been signed by Mr. Griffith in *blank.** '

That the magistrates agreed to send her back to
Manchester in a chaise; and that letters were
written, signed by the magistrates, to *Mr. Griffith*
⸻ and

---

* This is not at all improbable, as it is well known to
have been a practice for warrants, for the apprehension of
accused individuals, to be signed in blank, and left with
the clerk, ready to be filled up, in the absence of the justice, though they purported to be granted *on oath, taken in*
the presence of the magistrate... Thus was the liberty of the
subject liable to be wantonly sported with, and rendered
subservient to the most sinister purposes.

and *Mr. Hallows.* Says, she arrived at Manchester about eight o'clock, and was left by the overseer at Mr. Hallows's house. That Mr. and Mrs. Hallows being from home, she waited a considerable time for their return, when Mrs. Hallows *told her to go about her business, that she had neither bed nor money for her.* At this juncture, she was so far advanced in pregnancy, that she was frequently seized with the pains peculiar to that situation, and much enfeebled. That the night on which she was turned out of Mr. Hallows's house, was *cold* and *rainy.* That she wandered about with her three children, in search of a lodging, whilst she was able to stand, till at last, she, and her little ones, sat down upon some wet steps in Jackson's-row, when the cries of her children brought to her assistance a poor woman, who compassionately gave up her bed to her and her children, otherwise she thinks she must have died. Further says, being then too weak to be removed without assistance;—on the following morning, Mr. Hallows gave her a ticket on Mr. Edgley for three shillings, and a room was taken for her in Queen-street; but, continuing in a weak state, she was put to bed, and the women lodgers, who were in the same house, looked after her children; that Mr. Hallows was applied to again for relief, when he sent her two shillings and six-pence; that on the Tuesday following Mr. Hallows called himself, and, finding her in bed, asked, whether she was lighter? she answered, no, but that she was very bad. Says, that he called the following day, and insisted on her being removed to the poor-house; that he was much enraged, and very abusive, telling her, that she had called at Mr. Paynter's office, and shewn the pass which had been given to her. Says, she told Mr. Hallows, if Mr. Paynter had any knowledge of it, it must have been from the magis-

K   trates

trates at Stockport, as she herself had never mentioned it to him, when he passionately answered,
" *Madam, I'll make you find it so.*" Says, at this
time she had had a midwife attending her for some
time on that day, as well as the day before, but
Mr. Hallows wished her to get up, and walk to
the poor-house ; on which it was declared by the
female lodgers, that she was unable to walk, and
that it was very *improper to have her taken out of.
her bed ;* that Mr. Hallows at length consented to
send for a carrying chair, and in that situation she
was conveyed to the poor-house. Further says,
*that she continued in labour until the Sunday morning
following, when she was delivered of a* DEAD CHILD,
which, as well as her present indisposition, she at-
tributes solely to the ill treatment she had received.

What heart, possessing the common feelings of
nature, can be unmoved at a recital of such com-
plicated distress? A wretched mother, borne down
at once with *cold, hunger,* and the PAINS OF LA-
BOUR, wandering with her little ones through the
streets, without food, or a place of shelter from the
rude and chilling blasts of a winter's night, is, indeed, a picture, at which humanity may shed her
tenderest tear. But it is unnecessary for me to
enlarge on so distressful a circumstance ; the
sufferings of this woe-worn and modest claimant
will, I am sure, find a place for pity in every feeling breast.

I ought to observe, that this poor woman was
confined to her bed-room near three months after
delivery ; that at the time she gave me the foregoing relation, she had lain-in many weeks, yet she
was so enfeebled, as to render assistance necessary
to support her while she made the above declaration.

As

As a confirmation in part of the truth of the aforementioned narrative, I have here subjoined a copy of her examination, taken at Stockport.

Cheshire, ⎰ Betty Pike, wife of William Pike,
to wit. ⎱ late of Manchester, was taken before us, three of his Majesty's justices of the peace acting for the said county of Chester, the 19th day of November 1794;

" Who on her oath says, that her husband, herself, and family, have for some time past lived in Manchester aforesaid, and that her husband left her about six weeks ago. Says, she has since made frequent applications to Mr. Hallows, the overseer of the poor, for relief for herself and family ; that he always refused giving her any, until she should receive a certificate from Baslow, in the county of Derby ; that the certificate not coming, she complained again to Mr. Hallows, who then told her, *" she must go fetch it herself,"* and gave her a walking pass, for that, he said, " was all he could do for her." She observed to Mr. Hallows, that she had no shoes, and he gave her a ticket.

That on waiting upon Mr. Hallows for the pass, Mr. Hallows not being at home, Mrs. Hallows gave her one for Baslow, with TWO SHILLINGS, and desired her not to shew it to any one, except the officers in the respective towns through which she had to pass, for relief, and by all means to destroy it before she arrived at Baslow, *and not to mention it to the overseer at Baslow, and not to say to any one that she had given her* TWO SHILLINGS, Says, she does not know the place of her settlement. BETTY PIKE."

Sworn before us, CHA. PRESCOT,
JNO. PHILLIPS,
GEO. HYDE CLARKE.

BENJAMIN HODGES, *late of the New-market, Manchester*, died a widower about the latter end of April 1791, leaving five children. At the time of his death he had a house very decently furnished, and had many outstanding book debts due to him, but was indebted to several people in small sums of money. As the creditors could not agree upon who should administer, or how the effects should be disposed of, it so happened that Mr. Unite, as overseer, was called into the house the day after the funeral, when he took an inventory of the furniture,—and the orphan children were placed out in the following manner. Mr. Paterson, of the Bridgewater-arms, took the eldest; Solomon Chadwick, the deceased's wife's brother, was to receive one shilling and nine-pence per week from the township, for the support of the second; John Marshall, two shillings per week with the third; Peter Lawson, two shillings per week with the fourth; and Robert Farrar, three shillings per week with the youngest child.

It appears that Mr. Unite left two women in care of the furniture, and afterwards brought Mr. Walker, an appraiser and auctioneer, who made another inventory, and also an appraisement of the goods. On enquiry, (in the course of this investigation,) Mr. Walker says,—*he thinks the valuation* was about forty pounds, and that he delivered the inventory to Mr. Unite—that he afterwards sold part of the goods, and paid the money to Mr. Unite, but the goods sold so low, that Mr. Unite thought he *could sell them better*, and therefore he left off.

It is ascertained, *by the testimony of purchasers*, that amongst the furniture, the following articles were sold, of which Mr. Unite has not yet produced an account.

Best

	£.	s.	d.
Best bedstocks and furniture	3	17	0
Children's bed ditto and ditto	1	1	0
Corner cupboard	0	18	0
Painted ditto	0	15	0
Knife box, 2s. 6d. spade and bellows, 3s.	0	5	6
Frying-pan and oak stand	0	3	0
Grate and oven	1	11	6
Looking-glass	0	9	0
Large mug, tea pot, and safe	0	5	9
	£9	5	9

As to the remaining part of the goods, it has hitherto been impossible to learn to *whom sold*—or to *what amount*—or *what remained on hand,* except, that it has since been *discovered,* that Mr. Unite sold an *engine for making reeds,* and other working tools, to Bartholomew Reeves, for TWENTY-FIVE POUNDS, and a *bureau and bookcase,* for SIX POUNDS, which monies Mr. Unite appears to have actually received; and to have ordered the books and papers to be tied in a handkerchief, with a striped silk gown belonging to Hodges, and to be taken to his house:

The person, who attended Hodges' family in his illness which immediately preceded his death, and was afterwards entrusted with the care of the furniture until the time of the sale, at which she was present; Says, that Mr. Unite called upon her just before the meeting held at the Bull's-head, in November 1794, on the subject of my charges, to ask her some questions respecting Hodges' sale, when he told her, *" that he had delivered over his accounts to Mr. Horsfall, and that they were calling upon him again ;"* but upon her telling him that he had not delivered over the *books of accounts, and papers, and the striped silk gown,* which she had carried to his house,

house, he said, " *damn it, they got under some other books, and got out of the way—that he had kept the gown about a twelvemonth, when he sold it for half a guinea.*"

MR. UNITE,

in account with the estate of the late BENJ. HODGES.

To the different articles of furniture above enumerated, and *proved to have been sold,* amounting to 40 16 3

By Mr. Unite's petty expences*,
  amounting to about 3 14 6

By cash paid *twelve months after Hodges's death,* to one of his creditors, in part of a debt of £ 17 .... 5 5 0

1791, June 1st, do. Mr. Unite paid Mr. Horsfall on this account 10 0 0

                           —————18 19 6

                      £21 16 9†

It now remains for Mr. Unite to account for the above balances, as well as for the remainder of the goods, which were of *considerable value.*

It appears from certain proceedings in Bow-street, that Mr. Milne has been actively engaged in the attempt to extricate Mr. Unite from his aukward predicament, and I sincerely wish that their joint

---

* The funeral expences were paid by the friends of the deceased.

† It has been attempted to *excuse* Mr. Unite from seventeen pounds of the above balance, by saying that he stands debtor in the town's books for that sum since the year 1791; but, I am well informed, that the sum in the town's books is for *cash actually advanced* to Mr. Unite by a late church-warden, and *not on this account.*

joint efforts had been crowned with success; but, I cannot help observing, that *the charge so seriously made against him, by the Associated Ley-payers—the " gentle jog" I gave him in the Chester, paper — the proceedings at the Bull's-head meeting, and my subsequent publication*—have not yet been sufficient to bring him forward to satisfy the public mind on this subject.—Surely this *fifth* publication will rouse the Ley-payers from their lethargy, and animate them to *claim—demand—* and *insist* upon, an immediate correction of these parochial abuses.

The following is a similar examination, yet attended with circumstances of a still more distressing and aggravating nature.

PEGGY WHITELEY, who resided with her parents many years in *Chapel-walks*—a family well known as to their general character, and held in repute—after the death of her parents, she rented a house in the same neighbourhood, and (before the facts disclosed in this publication happened) lived in credit, and saved money.

This examinant saith, on the 4th of June 1790, Mr. Unite, as overseer of Manchester, with two men, seized her, and hawled her by force—, without shoes, stockings, or any covering whatever, save her linen and undercoat—and dragged her to the workhouse—where he gave orders to have her *chained to the floor*, and that no person should be permitted to see her ; that she was a lunatic. Says, she remained till the following day, when the governor, Mr. Taylor, paid attention to her story, and relieved her ;—finding her (as he has since expressed himself) perfectly sensible and intelligent. Says, on the afternoon of her release, she was ordered to be taken by Mr. Unite to the New Bayley—*in the same nearly naked situation.*

she

she was brought into the workhouse; and that she
imagined this was done to favour Mr. Unite's design, that she might have the appearance of a lunatic, as Mr. Unite had represented her, which
seemed with the magistrates to have its desired effect; for in that situation she was not permitted to
speak for herself.—It should be noticed, that Mrs.
Taylor, the governess of the workhouse, lent her
a *cloak* to cover her, and an *old pair of shoes,*
that she might not appear so indecent through the
streets on the road to the New Bayley—but, upon
Mr. Unite's observing it, he was highly offended
at the governess—and ordered the *cloak* and *shoes*
to be taken from her, *and to be conveyed there in this
almost naked situation!* That on her return from the
New Bayley, she continued in the workhouse till
the Tuesday following, when a plan was formed in
the house that she might escape—as her confinement appeared to *all* who had seen and heard her
story,—to be *an act of the most severe cruelty!*—
Says, that Mr. Unite had the key of her house,
and made a search for her property, where he
found, *tied up in a purse,* EIGHTY-EIGHT GUINEAS
—TEN CROWN PIECES and THREE DOLLARS;—
that he likewise found *thirteen silver spoons, marked E & K—two silver table spoons, marked M W,*
being the initials of her name—a pair of silver tea
tongs—a silver cream jug, marked also M W, and
a pinchbeck watch—and that Mr. Unite took
away with him the above *cash, plate,* &c. *

On the 8th day of March, Mr. Unite and a Mr.
Walker, appraiser and auctioneer, disposed of all
her furniture; in a short time after she called on
Mr.

* I cannot help observing here, that some time ago I
made enquiry of a very respectable broker, who attended
the sale, and who told me, that the house was well furnished—that she had not less than thirty mahogany chairs,
with

Mr. Unite, much distressed for want of meat and clothes, and earnestly entreated him to advance her some part of her money for her present relief —that she begged Mr. Unite would tell her the nature of her offence—but that he made her no answer;—that the following is a part of her goods, which, she has since heard, was sent *from her house to Mr. Unite's,* viz. *her best new bed, with chints curtains—an elegant chest of drawers—with pictures, chairs, china, looking-glasses, &c.* without any account being delivered of the same.

This examinant, Peggy Whiteley, says, that she made application to Mr. Unite for the chest of drawers; as they were of her father's making, she was desirous of keeping them in remembrance of him : but Mr. Unite put her off, by telling her, it would have an odd appearance the taking them out of his house again, but that *she might get them valued herself, and he would pay her for them.* Says, at the time she waited upon Mr. Unite, she saw the *part of her china in use at Mr. Unite's house*— and *that her glasses were on his sideboard —* and a *picture,* which was a much-admired painting of a battle in Cromwell's time, hung up in the hall. Says, Mr. Unite has since told her, that she might thank her brother for her present distress, and if *she did not keep silent, it would cause her brother to be punished !* That a cellar was engaged for her to live in, in Thomas's-street, where she was obliged to *wind yarn for her livelihood*—and having

L   to

with three or four beds, and other goods in proportion. He likewise added, that *many of the best goods* (according to the information he received at the sale) WERE NOT TO BE SOLD BY AUCTION—*and that he afterwards learned*—that one picture, now in Mr. *Unite's* house, was said to be sold for two shillings and six-pence, that he should have been glad to have been the purchaser at two guineas, but that it was worth more money, *and that a great variety of goods were taken to Mr. Unite's house.*

to pay two shillings and three-pence per week
rent, *she was nearly starved to death—having no assistance whatever from Mr. Unite, though he was
then in possession of all her property.*—Says, that
Mr. Kay, a tradesman, who lived in the upper part
of the house, recognised her features, and enquired
the reason of her distress, which, on repeating, he
begged her to make herself as decent as possible,
and to call upon Mr. Whittaker, attorney, and re-
late her case ;—that *Mrs. Kay* lent her some
clothes, and she waited on Mr. Whittaker, to
whom she related Mr. Unite's conduct ; but says,
she concealed from Mr. Whittaker, her *dark—
damp—and pitiful habitation*—that she did not tell
him, at that time, she *had not tasted meat for three
days*—that she *was pennyless*—without *fire—can-
dles*—or *victuals ;*—that she was afraid of mentioning her *extreme poverty*—imagining, if *all were
told*—there would appear too great an *improbabil-
ity in the relation* for any *human mind to credit !*—
so that she kept the *keen* and *pressing story of hunger to herself !*—Says, that Mr. Whittaker paid a
compassionate attention to the account which she
gave of Mr. Unite's conduct, and promised her
every assistance in his power. That Mr. Whittaker called upon Mr. Unite, and asked him the
reason for *his turning her out of her house, and taking to himself her plate, cash, and goods.* That Mr.
Unite told Mr. Whittaker, that he had been informed by her brother, that she was not sound in
mind, and that it was very likely she might become
chargeable to the town. Mr. Whittaker asked, if
she owed any thing for rent ? to which she answered, that she was punctual in every quarterly
payment. Here, Mr. Whittaker appealed to Mr.
Unite's *feelings*, and painted the atrocity of his
crime—when Mr. Unite's reply was—*" that she
was a bad woman—and that he knew many who had
been*

been connected with her."—Says, on hearing this account from Mr. Unite,—she burst into tears—when Mr. Whittaker called him *a villain*—and asked him to mention one person that he knew had been connected with her. Mr. Unite replied, that "*he knew many, but they were soldiers in the last regiment, and had left the town.*" Says, Mr. Whittaker threatened Mr. Unite with a lawsuit, and that he, Mr. Whittaker, had a conference with Mr. Bayley upon this business—but does not know what passed, only that Mr. Whittaker told her, that *Mr. Unite's conduct ought to be made public.* Mr. Unite afterwards *waited upon her, and insisted on her stopping the proceedings against him.* Says, Mr. Unite promised to return her *clothes* and *money*—and that her extreme poverty obliged her to consent. Says, she thinks one of *Mr. Milne's clerks* was with him, and that they had a paper with them, *ready prepared,* which she signed, but the contents she is unacquainted with—and she was likewise made to promise never TO MENTION TO MR. WHITTAKER the *reason of her discontinuing the action.*—Says, that Mr. Unite, *as she had* (to use his own words) *for ever lost her character in the town,—if she would leave it—she might depend upon his being a friend to her.*—Thus deprived of her property, and of the means of getting a livelihood, she existed in a miserable situation nearly six months,—with scarcely half clothes—being deprived of the following articles, which were in her house, when Mr. Unite took possession, viz.

Eighteen gowns, silk and prints ;
Four black cloaks ;
Two woollen ditto ;
Nineteen aprons, caps,—stockings, in proportion;
Twelve shifts ;
Eighteen pairs of sheets,—blankets, &c. in proportion.

Says,

Says, by this ill treatment, her health was so much impaired, that she applied to Dr. Percival.

Says, that in consequence of the promise she made Mr. Unite to discontinue the action against him, he paid her *one hundred and fifteen pounds*, which is the whole amount received for her *cash, plate, furniture,* &c. and that she never saw any inventory of the sale.

On the perusal of the foregoing narrative every reader must be struck with indignant astonishment, and will, doubtless, ask himself this question —*could an outrage like this be perpetrated in a land where the liberty and security of the subject are held inviolate ?*—It is really so unaccountably atrocious, and comprises so much fraud, cruelty, and oppression, that had it not been a fact completely substantiated by concurrent testimony, it might have been deemed incredible.

Allowing this poor and much-injured woman to have absolutely laboured under a mental derangement—was it a justifiable proceeding to force her *from* her peaceable home—to drag her like a felon through the streets—to take her to prison—to accuse her falsely with incontinency—to obtain her signature to an instrument which was previously prepared (when he had accused her of insanity)—to demand her secrecy, on pain of having her brother punished—to make proposals (when his conduct towards her had come to the knowledge of Mr. Whittaker) for her to leave the town, and in consequence *to be received into his friendship*—to despoil her of her property, and to expose her to all the bitterness of want?—This was a chain of cruelty, ill calculated to heal her infirmity, and to restore lost reason.

It

It is a lamentable consideration, that these *receptacles for the poor;*—these great and benevolent institutions, should be made subservient to the worst of purposes.—Various are the instances within our knowledge, where *private* mad-houses have been established, not for the laudable purpose of restoring to miserable lunatics " *their lost and scattered senses*"—but to be the engines of the most foul conspiracies against the peace, happiness, and fortunes, of individuals.—Numberless unhappy victims, in the full enjoyment of their senses, have been immured in these infernal mansions for life—on a false plea of insanity!—And, I wish I could say, that it was impossible for a *parish workhouse* to be so wickedly perverted—but, when I have it from indisputable authority, that a *virtuous* and *respectable* woman—in the full possession of reason, and capable of fulfilling every domestic duty, is made a sacrifice to the depravity of a *debauched* and *unprincipled* husband—and kept in a parish workhouse as a lunatic—it becomes then a duty, which humanity dictates, to bring such dark and cruel proceedings to light—and as long as such diabolical practices exist—I trust the authors will ever be exposed!

GRINDRED's Sale, *Salford.* Grindred became chargeable to Manchester, and was removed to the workhouse. At his death, his goods were sold—but there does not appear any entry made whatever. *Mr. Kinnaston, constable of Salford,* says, they netted little more than what paid his debts—but that Mr. Unite had a *clock*, which he does not know *how* accounted for.

As

As every effort of mine to obtain a sight of Mr,
Unite's *books*, during his *deputy constableship*, has
proved ineffectual, I shall only make a few general
remarks on the *abuses of his office*,—not doubt-
ing but the Ley-payers will soon see the necessity
of these, as well as all other town's books, being,
as the act directs, " *kept in some safe place for the
inspection of the public.*"

The large folio constables' book, containing the
whole of those accounts for the last twenty years,
is said to be *lost*, so that it is impossible for me to
make a retrospective comparison with accuracy.

The *constables' accounts*, from Easter 1792 to
Easter 1793, *exceeded* £1080; though, if I re-
member rightly, a few years ago, they did not
amount to one-third, including the salaries of the
deputy-constable and beadles, with the conveyance of *thieves* and *vagrants—passes—firemen—*
SCAVENGERS, &c. The public were not then
burthened with a POLICE TAX, *for which such
enormous sums have been collected*—and which, should
have operated in reduction of the constables' yearly expenditures,—but, there seems of late to have
been *a general dread of investigation*—insomuch,
that *one* of the constables not long ago *voted* against
the auditing of his own accounts! From a chain
of such-like circumstances, there appears something very *unfair* in the *practices* of that department.

The method of having the *deputy-constables' accounts* cursorily read over at the Collegiate church
quarterly—without the permission of an inspection
afterwards—is a practice very liable to imposition.

At one of these quarterly meetings which I attended, after the recital of a long list of the deputy-
constable's disbursements—I waited some time in
expectation

expectation of hearing the credit side read—but to my great astonishment I was informed by M*. *Whittaker* (who has *of late* attended as *advocate* for Mr. Unite) *that there did not appear to have been any cash received during that quarter!* As the *credits* in the constables' *yearly accounts usually* exceeded one-fourth of the *yearly disbursements*—I confess, I thought it somewhat curious, that at the only two meetings I ever attended on this occasion, there did not appear any monies to have been received.

Some time ago, a friend of mine, who was present at one of these quarterly meetings, was not a little surprised at hearing a credit given for *two shillings and six-pence* or *three shillings and six-pence* for the *net proceeds of the sale of* TWO HORSES! And what added to his astonishment was—that many very extraordinary *debits* and *credits* passed—without a single question being asked.

On my enquiry concerning these *two horses*—I was informed they were left by a *gang of coiners*, at the *Red Lion Inn, in Salford*; who, being suspected, ran off.—The horses were sold by public auction in St. Ann's-square, as follows :

One horse for	4	7	0					
The other	7	15	0					
				12	2	0		
Innkeeper's bill	5	15	0					
Hostler	0	10	6					
				6	5	6		
				£5	16	0		

It should be remarked, that during the long time that these horses were in *Mr. Hartley's stables, in Salford*—they were regularly *hacked out*. It appears from Mr. Unite's notes to the hostler—

that

that they were *lent,* or *hired* out, for a week at a
time ;—that a person called upon Mr. Hartley, to
hire a horse for Knutsford races—Mr. Hartley not
having one of his own, sent him to Mr. Unite, and
the person immediately returned with a note from
Mr. Unite for the delivery of one of the said horses.
Instead of being put into condition for sale, they
were nearly broken down with hard riding.

The billeting of soldiers, for which *Mistress*
UNITE receives *thirty pounds* a year, may justly
be termed a *snug sinecure,* as the whole of the billets for *one week* may be easily written from the
publicans'. returns for that space; in less than ten
minutes ;—and how easy would it be for one of
the beadles (as there is, or should be, always one
out of the *three* to attend the police office) to
deliver billets when applied for.   —

Viewing the *nature* of this department in a variety of instances, a woman of any delicacy of
sentiment would shrink from the practice !

Though the barracks have taken away the principal attention required in billeting—as well as a
great burthen from the publicans—yet, there are
many publicans who labour *at this time* under the
most *severe hardships* from the *conduct of Mrs. Unite.*
Of this I shall only mention *one* or *two* instances ;
—without insinuating any malevolence on her part;
I shall leave the reader to form his own opinion
from the following circumstances :

Some few months ago, the publicans of Manchester were waited upon for a *subscription to pay
off Mr. Unite's debts*—which subscriptions were
individually from ten shillings and six-pence to
one pound one shilling, and some names were said
to be on the list for five pounds five shillings,
which procured him a very considerable sum of
money.—Amongst these publicans it was *unfortun-
ately* observed by a *landlady*—" that if Mr. Unite

were

were to go less to Peter Fearnhead's—Mrs. Unite were to dress more becoming her situation, and to be otherwise less extravagant—there would be no occasion to beg money from publicans to pay his debts."— She was then given to understand—*that Mr. Unite had great power—that a guinea given to him would not be lost—that Mr. Unite would see by the sub-scriptions* WHO *were his friends ;*—but, having too much spirit to buy, or court, Mr. Unite's favours, at the expence of a guinea—she was soon after-wards complimented with *five men* and *five horses,* though, from every information in my power, I could not find at that time more than *twenty horses billeted on the whole of the publicans in Manchester !*

This house, for the last *six months,* has been distressed by having considerably more *soldiers* and *horses* than their proportionate share—at this peri-od, January 1796, they have no less than EIGHT MEN and EIGHT HORSES *on billet*—though there is not *a* HORSE for every *two* public houses through the town.—The *landlord* at the *Crown and Anchor,* top of Dean's-gate, has been much in-jured by having more than his share of soldiers—though this house lies out of the way of busi-ness, the landlord has had nine men billeted on him at a time. On the 31st of December, 1795, he made application to Mrs. Unite, having *four men* and *four horses*—when she gave him very insulting lan-guage—threw the door in his face—and would not listen to his complaint.

The landlord afterwards made application to Mr. Thomas Richardson, and represented the hardship under which he laboured, by having more than his number of soldiers.—Mr. R. accompanied the landlord to the billet-office—having, as he said, some *influence* over Mr. Unite, beng the *first subscriber of* ONE GUINEA, at *Peter Fearnhead's,* towards the payment of his debts ;—but Mr. Unite

M   not

not being at home, their visit proved ineffectual.—
In the course of a few days afterwards, the landlord was sent for by Mr. Unite, who made the
wished-for regulation.

In the month of November last, I happened to
be at a public-house in the neighbourhood of the
Old-church—where the landlady had just made
out a weekly return of FOUR MEN AND FIVE
HORSES—and at the foot of the return she had
written " *bona fide—so many;*" but, instead of
this remark, having its desired effect, another *soldier* was sent to make the *men* and *horses* of equal
number. The circumstance of having FIVE MEN
AND FIVE HORSES on billet—at one house, is an
expence of more than *thirty shillings per week !*—
On the 22d day of December, curiosity led me to
enquire at TEN of the principal inns in town, where
I found neither *soldier* nor *horse*—and several of
them have had no HORSES *for many months !*

The *town* of SALFORD—*the share of which,
with Manchester, is every* SIXTH SOLDIER
AND HORSE, had not, at this time, ONE
HORSE billeted in the *whole* TOWN !!

The last billet-master (though he had a large
family to provide for) lost his office, by only receiving THREE-PENCE *for the billet of every
new-made soldier ;* whilst the office at this time is
filled with the most glaring, and almost *incredible
irregularities*, which, under the direction of *Mrs.
Unite*, pass with *impunity !*

The salaries for the joint offices of *deputy-constable* and *billet-master*, in *Mr. Wilford's* time, was
only thirty pounds per annum—there was then no
POLICE OFFICE, at the expence of *one hundred
and fifty pounds-per annum rent*—nor *were there so
many perquisites* as there now are—though the present salaries of Mr. and Mrs. Unite,—with house-
rent,

rent, amount to THREE HUNDRED AND THIRTY POUNDS a year!

In *Mr. Scholes's* constableship the salary was raised from £80. to £150. per annum, with this proviso—that *no perquisites whatever* should be received by the deputy-constable. Why is not this agreement put in force?—Mr. Unite has the same salary, with the addition of *house-rent*, and ought to account for *all* SUMMONSES *and* WARRANTS — SUNDAY FINES — STOLEN GOODS — COUNTY ALLOWANCES, &c. &c.—NO BRIBES should be taken in BILLETING—nor *presents received of any description from publicans*—nor should any *subscriptions be extorted from publicans, to pay the debts of a deputy-constable* (however contracted) *nor should any monies be borrowed from publicans— as it is but too natural to expect great indulgencies, by way of interest, where the principal is in a doubtful state!*

As the POLICE OFFICE is entailed on the town *for ever*, at the enormous rent of *one hundred and fifty pounds per annum*—it ought to be made to answer some useful purpose ;—it might be converted into different apartments, for *collectors, overseers,* &c. &c.—there might be an office for paupers to receive their tickets—and another office for the cashier, without harrassing the poor by long attendances for their tickets in one part of the town, and afterwards for payment in another ;—which is generally the loss of a day before they receive their mite.

The *constable, beadles,* and *billet-mistress,*—and *every servant* belonging to the town, should pay that attendance which the nature of their office requires ;—at present this *large mansion* seems of little or no use, except for *private balls*—or to let off as a *lodging-house,* for the benefit of Mr. Unite,

in

in addition to his *enormous* salaries and perquisites.

I should likewise beg leave to recommend to
the magistrates, to put a stop to the practice of
taking to the New Bailey prison, persons for *triv-
ial offences,* not cognizable by law—it is giving a
constable an *arbitrary* and *despotic power*—both to
imprison and to set at *liberty* at will;—but we have
instances of both Mrs. *and Miss Unite having as-
sumed* to themselves the *office and functions of
magistracy, by ordering the imprisonment of individuals of their own authority!*

The following specimen of such conduct in the
young lady, deserves reciting:

One *Henry O'Neal,* servant to *Lieutenant Fox,*
of the 122d regiment of foot, but now of the roy-
als, (in October last) was called to by Miss Unite,
while passing near the bottom of King-street, into
the *police office,* under the pretext of asking him a
question—when she caused him to be seized by
the beadles—and taken to the New Bailey, where
he was imprisoned THREE DAYS!—The only crime
laid to his charge was, that he had spoken rather
ludicrously of Miss Unite, and the son of Mr. R.—
a fruiterer;—after this confinement, he was discharged by order of *Mr. Unite!*

Some time ago, application was made to Mr.
Unite, by a gentleman, who suspected a female
visitor of good family from Liverpool, with having
taken various articles out of his house. Mr.
Unite, in the absence of this lady, opened with a
false key, her trunk—where he found inclosed in
her work-bag, about twelve yards of muslin, and a
variety of other articles, which were owned, of
considerable value. This was most certainly an
aggravated offence, of which several servants had
been suspected before any suspicion fell upon this
lady.

Mr.

Mr. Unite conveyed her to the New Bailey, where she continued a day and night; at last a Captain * * * * made intercession with the prosecutor,—who *receiving back his property*—and on obtaining her note for near twenty pounds for monies advanced on her account, &c. the prosecutor *sent Mr. Unite a note for her discharge.*

Had this woman been found guilty *of being poor,* who then would have pleaded in extenuation of her offence—or would, under circumstances so strong, have lent an helping hand to have saved her from merited punishment ? It would seem, as though *money, aided by beauty,* were advocates sufficiently powerful to disarm public justice ;—by their assistance *a crime of the blackest dye,* can indulgently be overlooked;—while a poor, miserable being, urged by the keen pressure of hunger, to a comparatively slight violation of the law—would have been commited to a *loathsome prison—hard galling fetters—and, on conviction,—to banishment for life!* This woman's crime was not the result of necessity—but actual depravity of heart—yet she received every *favour* and *indulgence* during the time of her imprisonment, and enjoyed *(for many weeks afterwards)* " *the pampered luxuries of a governor's table.*"

This too much verifies the observation of Shakespear—

—————————————————" Plate sin *with gold,*
" And the strong lance of justice, hurtless breaks :
" Arm it *in rags,*—a pigmy's straw doth pierce it."

The following very curious account respecting Mr. Hallows, I had thought to have reserved for another publication,—but, as he seems very importunate for the payment of a considerable sum of money, from the town, I have now introduced it, that the present overseers may make the necessary enquiries,

enquiries, and set off the same against any demand he may pretend to have against the town.

The churchwardens, in 1793, agreed with one Kelly, to make brick on the land near the workhouse, at nine shillings and six-pence per thousand, under the inspection of Mr. Rowland ;—some few days after the agreement, a dispute arose between Rowland and Kelly, when Kelly requested Mr. Locke, the then churchwarden, to pay him the money for brick-making, without its going through Mr. Rowland's hands, which was agreed to. Some time after, Mr. Rowland and Kelly met, by chance, at Messrs. Jones's bank, where Mr. Rowland observed Kelly present Mr. Lock's check for twenty-seven pounds, and was not a little surprised on knowing that the work done did not amount to *one-half* of that sum. Mr. Rowland made an immediate application to Mr. Locke, who ordered Kelly's account to be examined.—Mr. Hallows attended on the part of Mr. Locke, and it was clearly proved, that Kelly had received from Mr. Locke ONE HUNDRED AND FIFTEEN POUNDS AND EIGHT-PENCE!—*more than he had earned*, as per the following account, settled by *Mr. Rowland, Kelly,* and *Hallows.*

To carting clay, back of the workhouse	60	6	6
To levelling, as per agreement	26	5	0
To ditto, in front	17	2	6
To casting clay adjoining the house	14	2	6
To ditto in the intended street	29	2	6
To wheeling from the front of the house	38	0	0
To work	6	2	6
£	191	1	6

Brought forward 191 1 6
By cash received by Kelly
  from Mr. Locke...................... 306 2 2
To balance, overdrawn Mr.
  Locke, as per Kelly's account 115 0 8

£ 306 2 2 £ 306 2 2

After this account had been adjusted, Kelly entered into an engagement to continue the making of the brick at nine shillings and six-pence per thousand—and to STOP *two shilllings and six-pence for every thousand made, to pay off the money he had overdrawn from Mr. Locke.*—The management of this concern was afterwards given to Mr. Hallows, who *promised to keep a strict watch over Kelly's conduct,* and particularly in the *stopping of the half-crown* for every thousand bricks made.—Mr. Hallows, at this time, had proposals made to him (as the brick-making business was very low) to make them at seven shillings and six-pence per thousand— "*counted out, workable brick;*"—yet Kelly was suffered to proceed in *making* and *kilning* such *brick as would not, when burnt, pay the duty !* At the end of the season, *Kelly disappeared,* and is since gone abroad, as a soldier.—It now remains with Mr. Hallows, *to give an account of his stewardship, —and to shew the public his accounts.*

On a moderate computation, there appears to have been near *one million* of bricks, made at nine shillings and six-pence per thousand, which should have been "*counted out workable brick from the kiln,*" as per agreement left with Messrs. Milne and Sergeant;—instead of which, they were counted on the ground when moulded — and many THOUSANDS put into the kiln *spoiled* by the weather, being moulded too early in the season;
in

in this shameful manner was the contract executed,
that scarcely one-half of the bricks were either
used or sold; great quantities, I am informed, have
been buried in the foundation of the walling
round the poor-house;—and there remained, some
time ago, a miserable sample of above *one hundred
thousand bricks* (out of *one kiln*, which at first contained *only* one hundred and ninety thousand)
which were not worth carrying away!—In this
shameful manner the property of the Ley-payers of
Manchester has been sported with.

As it is whispered that Mr. Hallows is again
coming into office, it may be necessary to caution
the *young* and *unsuspecting*, of the various and dis-
graceful arts he has had recourse to, in order to extort money in cases of bastardy.—One method is, to
call upon persons as the *reputed* fathers of children, under the mask of friendship, when he will
probably introduce the story of some woman being pregnant, whom he has prevented from going
before the magistrates to father the child ; here
the usual complimentary business of *"Hush money"*
is distantly introduced. Should this conversation
happen with a single man, who does not betray
much fear—he will, probably, tell him, that the
business shall be settled for five pounds ;—but if it
should be pointed to a married man—he seldom
fails mentioning the inconvenience attending the
exposure before the magistrates, and the consequent
uneasiness it may occasion at home, from its being
made public ;—in such a case his expectations are
raised *in proportion to the delicacy of their situation!*
I have it likewise from undoubted authority, that
different gentlemen have been applied to for
" *Hush money,*" *as the pretended fathers of the* SAME
child !
A gentleman, with whom I have a slender ac-
coming

quaintance, was some time ago waited upon by Mr. Hallows, who told him, *a female connection* of his had turned out a *prolific one;*—unaccustomed to Mr. Hallows's proceedings, he came immediately to a settlement, and he received Mr. Hallows's *written indemnification* from every expence, for NINE GUINEAS. Though this appeared *reasonable* indeed, and well settled—it was to a " *dead certainty*" *all profit,* for the child expired the day before;—and, at the time the settlement took place, was *actually*—IN ITS COFFIN! *

The following circumstance, I should have thought, would have deterred him in future from such-like proceedings: he, some time ago, called at the Infirmary, and enquired for one of the surgeons, by whom he pretended a woman in the town was pregnant: the surgeon happened, at this time, to be engaged in the amputation of a leg;—Mr. Hallows waited some time, with great impatience, when the surgeon was again enquired after, who came down with stripped-up sleeves, and nearly covered with blood:—Mr. Hallows introduced the *old story of pregnancy*—but, added he,—" *this is a particular and very unfortunate case, for the child is born blind, and it will be a heavy charge upon you while it lives*"—to which the surgeon, very deliberately replied, " *it may be so, Mr. Hallows— but I am not to be duped—old birds are not to be caught with chaff—and by G-d—if I had the instruments here—that I have been using in the taking off a limb—I would take off both your ears, you scoundrel.*"— Hallows hastily disappeared — and the *blind child* has never since been *seen* or heard of.

I am sorry to observe, that *pregnant women belonging to other parishes,* after the removal order is made out, in order to prevent their children from gaining a settlement in this township, and FOUR-

TEEN

---

* This is cousin-german to Pinder's *elegant* story of a group of churchwardens " *eating a child!*"

TEEN SHILLINGS paid in the manner I have before mentioned, are very often dragged to the poorhouse by force—where I have heard of them being confined for several months, and actually for want of proper attention to the order; have been detained, and brought to bed in the house.

Some of these unfortunate women have had *logs of wood chained to their legs, to prevent their escape from confinement.*—This punishment depends upon the caprice of an overseer, which is very often equal to that inflicted on criminals charged with capital offences.—After child-birth, some have staid in the workhouse several months, at the expence of the town, and have been afterwards permitted to go at liberty—*as if no removal order had been made out!*

I am at a loss to conceive what plea can justify such treatment of these *unfortunate women.* I do not mean to stand forth the champion of prostitution—yet, I think much may be said in extenuation of many young and unsuspecting females. Instead then of increasing the misery to these already sufficiently afflicted victims, by imprisonment and harsh treatment, humanity would dictate towards them the exercise of pity and compassion—or at least an immediate removal to the residence of their friends, who are in such cases the most likely and the most eligible " *to throw the veil of human kindness over human frailty.*"—and to give that tenderness and attention to their situation, which they might not experience from others.

Amongst the various hardships which the poor lie under, from *unprincipled* and *wicked* overseers— surely nothing can equal that inhumanity of paying them their " *scanty pittance,*" with *base* and *counterfeit copper.* The Rev. Mr. John Griffith, late a magistrate, charged overseer Hallows, in a public company, with having purchased of a Mr. M——o,

M——o, ONE HUNDRED POUNDS *in copper of that 'description*, for FORTY POUNDS! and which he said had been paid to Manchester paupers.—— The cruelty practised towards the poor, in a traffic of this nature, where an overseer makes SIXTY PER CENT. *profit!* is so shameful and illegal a pro- ceeding, that it ought to be noticed by the magis- trates, and if it should appear that Mr. Hallows's colleague in office, was a party concerned, he ought to be dismissed as unworthy of public trust.

In consequence of a letter, which I received some time ago, (a copy of which I have here an- nexed) I was desirous of seeing Mr. Hallows's ac- counts for 1794, which he kept under the title of "EXTRAORDINARY PAYMENTS," but I soon found they were of too *extraordinary* a nature for my inspection!—The following account, pub- lished pages 16 and 17, in my Reply to Mr. Unite, is a specimen of some of Mr. Hallows's charges on journies—and shews his great *liberality* in the dis- tribution of the town's cash.

Nov. 4th. To expences TWO *journies to 'Radcliffe (on the same day).*	0	14	0
To expences (same day) to Bury, respect- ing George Isherwood's settlement	0	10	0
	£1	4	0

"To four men for taking, AND *the soldier in Newton-lane"*	0	6	0
*"*TO LIQUOR FOR THE SAME*"*	0	5	3
	£0	11	3

The latter charge of *eleven shillings and three- pence,* occasioned the following letter.

Mr.

Mr. Battye,

　　Sir,

　　　　　In looking over your *Reply to Mr.
Unite's advertisement,* we, the *under-named, observed
a statement of the overseers' accounts, concerning the
taking up the soldier. In page* 16*th of your Reply,
—it is there said—To four men for taking* AND *the
soldier in Newton-lane—and to liquor for the same—
total amount eleven shillings and three-pence.* As
we did not desire any *fee or reward for watching them
—we take this opportunity to let you and the committee know—that there was no money given, but two
shillings and one glass of liquor, which could not
be more than three-pence, it being our principle
only that led us into this business—and we think our-
selves imposed upon—by so much money* SAID *to be
given and expended.*

　　*If you think this worth your notice, please either to
call, or direct a line to No.* ——

　　We are your most obedient servants, &c.

　　If the public can give credit to the above letter,
where Mr. Hallows charges eleven shillings and
three-pence for two shillings and three-pence really paid, what confidence can be placed in the accuracy of his accounts? These men, whose names
I have omitted here, are at any moment ready to
establish the facts on oath.

　　The following is another sketch of a part of Mr.
Hallows's accounts, and will be a further specimen
of his charges, which appear to be rendered *quarterly to Mr. Edgley, the cashier,* on a few loose
sheets of paper, PINNED together, amounting to
near seven hundred pounds per annum, and which
abound with entries of the following nature, without any other *remarks* or *vouchers* for the payments.

　　　　　　　　　　　　　　　.*E. Holland*

	£.	s.	d.
E. Holland to London............	o	10	6
E. Douglas to ditto	o	10	o
Tattersall's wife & child, ditto	o	10	6
An appointment............	o	10	o
Ann Eves	o	5	o
M. Halstead	o	7	6
Fanny Robinson................	o	12	o

The three first payments are to *strangers*, with
only their names mentioned, *travelling to London*.
Had these people *actually* applied for relief—
THREE SHILLINGS—*instead of* THIRTY SHLLINGS
AND SIX-PENCE, would have been more than what
is usually given, as there are no less than six constables in seven miles, the distance from hence to
Stockport, where these people would, no doubt,
apply for relief;—as well as in every constable-
wick on the road to London.

Mr. Hallows's next charge is, " AN APPOINT-
MENT," *half a guinea!* but, *with whom?* or, on
what account? It is but simply just, that the particulars of this appointment should be specified—
even if it were of a *private nature*—being paid out
of the *public purse.* Ann Eves—Betty Allen—M.
Halstead—and Fanny Robinson, seem to have
been very liberally paid;—but it would have been
too *much trouble* to have said who these women
were—or where they were going; as they appear
only to have been relieved with *one pound four shillings and six-pence!*

Mr. *Unite*, on his paying the town's cash, is a
little more particular in his entries, than his brother
colleague;—though there appears, in his accounts,
no more certainty or honesty in his method of
making extraordinary payments, than there does
in Mr. Hallows's accounts, as appears by the following entry.

To

By cash paid to a COUNTRY OVERSEER, *for cash advanced* a POOR FAMILY *to a* TOWNSHIP in the NORTH RIDING OF YORK, *two pounds nineteen shillings !*

Let me ask any of the late church-wardens, if such kind of *evasive* entries had been made in their own *private accounts*, whether they would have passed unnoticed? As well might Mr. Unite have said, that he had paid the money to an overseer at *Calcutta* or *Madrass*, as in the *North Riding of York.*

Or, had the names of *John Nokes* or *Thomas Styles*— *John Doe* and *Richard Roe*—or, *Thomas Hickathrift* or *Jack the Giant-killer*, appeared in Mr. Unite's or Mr. Hallow's books, to have received money as *country overseers*, or *paupers*;— it would not have carried more *conviction* along with it, than the foregoing entry.

The following accounts are a few auxiliary charges, which serve to make up Mr. Hallows's very *extraordinary* expenditure.

	£.	s.	d.
1794. *To journey to Burbage and Morley, to serve notice of an appeal, took with me Mr. Milne, jun.*	3	7	6
To my journey to Stockport, respecting Carey's settlement	0	13	6
To removal of ditto	0	14	6
To journey to Rooden-lane and Blakeley	0	7	6
To ditto to Stayly Bridge to serve copy of an order*	0	13	6
To ditto to Ashton, to serve a summons in bastardy, and to visit Holt's family	0	13	6

To

* Whilst Mr. Hallows is this day going to *Stayley Bridge*, to serve the *copy of a bastardy order*—for which he charges 13*s*. 6*d*. Mrs. Hallows relieves *thirty strangers*, at home, said to be going to different parts of the kingdom, with £3. 18*s*.—On the *prior* and *subsequent* days of Mr. Hallows's journey, *only three people are relieved*.

To coach-hire to see Mr. Bayley, of Hope	0	7	6

To coach-hire to see Mr. Bayley, of Hope   0   7   6

*To expences going to Newcastle to see a lunatic ** 1   17   6

To journey to Heaton respecting Charles Davies's settlement 0   7   6

To ditto to Stockport ditto Lomas's ditto.... 0   10   0

To ditto to Rochdale, to serve R. Holt with a copy of a bastardy order 0   16   6

To journey respecting Burrow's settlement 2   10   0

To cash, with subpœna for THOMAS DUNN *(now in Lancaster for perjury)* 0   10   6

To ditto paid ——————— *by order of Justice Griffith* † 0   10   6

To my journey to Sandbach, respecting George Griffith's settlement, CHAISE HIRE, AND EXPENCES *for Mr. Serjeant and self* 7   14   6

To HORSE HIRE *for* MR. LOCKE, MR. EDGLEY, *and Mr. Hallows, to visit* NURSE CHILDREN ‡!! 0   12   0

                                            Tolls

---

  * In Mr. Hallows's absence (on a visit to the lunatic, from motives of *fellow-feeling*, no doubt) *thirty-nine strangers* are said to be relieved at home, on travel, in one day. And on his journey to Rochdale, respecting one Sanderson's settlement, *twenty-seven* are entered by *Mrs. Hallows*, as relieved; though on the *prior* and *subsequent* days of Mr. Hallows's journies, there are only *five* persons relieved on travel.

  † Why leave this entry blank?. was Mr. Griffith ashamed of the person he ordered the money to be paid to? —Mr. Hallows might have inserted the name of DUNN— as his name appears in different places, as a receiver of cash in this account of *"extraordinary payments"*—as well as the half-guinea given with his subpœna.—The purpose which this deluded wretch's service was intended to answer— sufficiently marks the *iniquity* of the application of this money.

  ‡ Whilst these *three gentlemen*, Mr. Locke, the head churchwarden—Mr. Hallows, the *deputy overseer*—and Mr. Edgley, the *cashier*—are ALL *visiting* NURSE CHIDREN at Altrincham—the Manchester poor, in the absence of Mr.

                                                Edgley

Tolls for the magistrates at the bridge...... o 6 8
Ditto for self and poor .... o 16 4
To EXPENCES *to* LANCASTER, *and re-*
turning, MR. MILNE, D. TOMLIN-
SON, *and* J. HALLOWS, CHARGED
IN GROSS! 24 14 6

The following I have inserted to shew the great
expence of reported journies relative to settlements.

1793. *To a journey to make enquiries about*
JOHN MARSH's *settlement* .... o 17 4
July 20. *To ditto to* LAWTON *, ASHTON,
NEWTON - IN - THE - WILLOWS, † *to*
PERFECT

Edgley, are unattended to. The CASUAL *poor is left as usual*
with Mrs. Hallows, who RELIEVED *this day* TWENTY-SEVEN
strangers on travel, with three pounds eleven shillings and
six-pence.

    * While Mr. Hallows is out on this journey to Lawton,
with Mr. Milne's clerk, at the expence of *four guineas and*
a half, more than FIFTY *persons* are *said* to be relieved
in *one* day, by Mrs. Hallows—*forty-six* are on travel to
different towns : and *nine* are *said* to be relieved with different sums, from one shilling to five shillings, as strangers;
with no other vouchers than their *names* opposite to the
respective sums paid.

    ☞ On June 3d, Mr. Hallows appears to have been at
Radcliffe, when Mrs. Hallows has made *twenty-three* entries
of *strangers* relieved, from one shilling to five shillings,
amounting to three pounds nine shillings. On the TWO
preceding days, Mr. Hallows being at home, there are only
seven relieved with *eleven shillings and six-pence*—and for
many days afterwards there are only *four entries* made. In
this year's accounts, there are many hundred extraordinary
payments,—*said* to be made—without troubling the cashier.
The hasty sketch of these accounts, I took by stealth—I
beg pardon of Mrs. and Mr. Hallows, for this interference
with their practice; but had I had time to have transcribed
the whole—the Ley-payers of Manchester should have been
furnished with copies, to have convinced them of the *proper*
application of the very heavy parochial taxes—and that the
deputy overseers are *year after year* superintended by *men of*
judgment.

    * This journey, being taken at the time of NEWTON
RACES,

Brought forward	o	17	4
PERFECT *the enquiry respecting* JOHN MARSH's *settlement, took with me* Mr. Lees, Mr. Milne's *clerk*	4	14	6
July 25. *To cash paid the* OVERSEERS *of* LAWTON	3	16	8
Oct. 15. *To cash for a journey to* LAWTON, *to make enquiries respecting* JOHN MARSH's *settlement,. took with me* Mr. Lees, Mr. Milne's *clerk*	3	10	0
Nov. 6. *To cash paid overseers of* LAWTON	3	17	0
£16	15	6

On the *second* journey to *Lawton*, the 20th of
July, it appears to have cost FOUR GUINEAS AND
A HALF ! for *two* persons travelling expences to
make an ENQUIRY PERFECT—and being
made so, Mr. Hallows FIVE days afterwards pays
to the *overseer of Lawton* three pounds sixteen
shillings—but on the 15th of October, the SAME
TWO repeat the same journey, to make PERFEC-
TION once more PERFECT—which then only cost
three pounds ten shillings. It appears that Mr.
Hallows, on making the last entry of three pounds
ten shillings, discovered that he had *forgot*, in his
last quarter's account given in to Mr. Edgley, to
give himself credit for the SECOND JOURNEY to
LAWTON, (at the race time) which he appears to
have *interlined* under the expence of *three pounds
ten shillings*—(being the THIRD journey to *Lawton)*
in a gross sum—FOUR GUINEAS AND A HALF !!

O   I can

RACES—it is natural to expect some crossing and jostling,
—it is very evident that it was better *jockeyship* than over-
seership—and it does not appear that Mr. Hallows has been
much out of pocket by making his *entries* at the *post.*

I can almost anticipate the reader's desire to know why this enquiry should have been so often made, and at so great an expence; or why *two* persons should be sent out on such an errand ;—to which I can only answer, that it is not only more *agreeable* to travel in company—but that it increases the expences to a *formidably looking sum ;—and swells no little the accounts of another nature.* ·,

In these quarterly accounts of Mr. Hallows's, are *interlineations* and *erasures*—sometimes a large sum is *forgotten* for *several months* to be entered! At other times there appear. erasures and remarks by a strange hand-writing—*"this sum is entered before,"* probably several months back, and yet *again* it makes its appearance! This convenient kind of forgetfulness—or rather this peculiar degree of *remembering* to *forget*—perhaps Mr. Hallow. borrowed from *high authority.*

It should be noticed through this year's account of 1794, whenever Mr. Hallows appears by the dates to have been *from home*, Mrs. Hallows appears to be then more *at home*—that lady's account of " *extraordinary payments*" are wonderful! There are more strangers relieved in his absence—than are generally relieved for many prior and subsequent days of his journies. It may probably seem curious, that total *strangers* to the town shoulp know when Mr. Hallows was from home ;—but such was the case, if what is recorded by Mrs. Hallows is to be credited, that from thirty to fifty *strangers*, are said to have received casual payments, generally on each day of Mr. Hallows's journies—which I will be bold to say, is a greater number than the present overseer's wife, in his absence, will relieve in any one month through the year. ·

,Mrs. Hallows appears, from her liberality to *travelling strangers*, through her whole *overseership—*

ship—to be the *milk of humanity*—her *profuse spirit*
of *benevolence*—would set the world a gadding !

The following is a specimen of Mr. Hallows's
charges on removals, which are numerous—there
appear no less than four hundred and forty-four
examinations respecting settlements, which took
place in *two years and a half* of Mr. Hallows's
overseership.

Removal of Martha Lee and two children to Withington	0	9	0
Ditto R. Evans, wife, and three children to Malpas	3	16	0
Horse hire	0	15	0
	4	11	0
Ditto Margaret Blinston to Chorley	1	10	6
Ditto Mary Smith and child to Timperley	0	11	0
Ditto Isherwood's wife and child to Bury	0	11	0
Ditto H. Dickinson to Sale *	0	10	0
Ditto Martha Garner to Cheadle	0	10	0
Ditto of Ann Butterworth to Moston	0	7	0
Ditto of J. Scott to Wilmslow	0	11	4
Ditto to Sheffield	6	6	0
Ditto Martha Fidler and five children, to Ashton *Ditto D. Chadwick, four ditto to ditto* }	1	18	3

The above charges are merely for expences on
these journies—every other expence relative to the
conveyance, with *cart* and *horse*, is contracted for
at five shillings per day, which is *not* included in
the above account. I find it has always been a
regular

* Though there are so many removals—at a great expence to most of the surrounding townships—Mr. Hallows
had an assistant, for which the town paid ten shillings per
week,

regular rule, for the expences of each journey to be particularized, and delivered to Mr. Hallows. I will not pretend to say—but from every information I have been able to collect, I think it utterly impossible, to find any *one* particular journey through the year, by comparing the cash *really* expended, with the amount of cash *actually* charged.

From a calculation which I have made, and from some pretty well authenticated information, I am very certain, that the same person who is now, and has been employed for some years, in this service, would convey the same number of paupers, to the same places of settlement, in the present year, for *considerably* less than ONE-HALF the expence charged to the town, under the direction of overseer Hallows.

The person with whom the contract is made for these removals, is a farmer, residing in the neighbourhood of Ashton, whom I accidentally met with a few days ago, and *taxed* with the very extravagant charge of one pound eighteen shillings and three-pence for *one journey*, with a *horse and cart*, from *Manchester* to *Ashton*, when the ingenuous farmer immediately declared, " that it was so short a journey to Ashton, and his farm being in the road, he made it a rule not to stop any where, but at home, for refreshment, either for himself or horse; and that he *never* had charged any thing, save the *turnpikes*, for a journey to Ashton, since he had done business with the overseers of Manchester."

Mr. Hallows, by his charge of £1. 18s. 3d. may not have consulted the amount of cash *really* paid, to form an exact estimate of profit on this journey; yet the odd *three-pence* sanctions the *appearance* of this *nicely* calculated charge, amounting to three shillings and five-pence a head, and eight-pence for the *turnpikes*.

Having,

Having, no doubt, sufficiently tired my readers with such a long list of Mr. Hallows's, *"extraordinary payments"*—let us now take a peep at him, as the competitor of Mr. Milne, in special pleading.

It has been a practice of some time standing—for the justices' clerk to receive a *guinea fee*—as *advocate* in cases of bastardy, and for such other offences as may have been brought before the magistrates.—This fee seems to me to be a kind of purchase, as well for their pleading, as their supposed influence with the bench—and I have often witnessed its wonder-working effect.

The business of *special pleading*, on these occasions, has also been pursued by Mr. Hallows, overseer; who has, in a variety of cases, practised with no little emolument to himself, and success to his client. An *artful tale*, told in a confidential manner to an *unsuspecting* bench, I have known to produce the wished-for success—even at a time when Mr. Milne, with all his *Ciceronian* eloquence, has pleaded in vain.

The following story may serve to elucidate, in some measure, the wonderful *virtue* of an *overseer's whisper.*

A case in bastardy came before a *late bench* of magistrates, when an order was made on the father of a child, who was a horse-dealer of some consequence, to pay three shillings per week—but, from a *false representation* (in a *whisper from the overseer*) as to the character of the woman—the order was reduced to *one shilling and six-pence per week!* The father, *truly sensible* of the obligation, made the following remark to the magistrate—*"you have made my ride easy,* for which you are at any time welcome to RIDE the best horse in my stable."

Such-like gratuities are so customarily received, by *men in office,* that even magistracy itself

(shame

(shame to the *indiscriminating race)* is sometimes ignorantly insulted.

After having taken a survey of Mr. Unite's *books*—I mean his *four small slips of paper,* which contain the whole of his accounts as overseer—it is but justice, due to him, to say,—(though it has been *maliciously* hinted that they remain unbalanced since the year 1791) they are, in point of compactness, equal, if not superior, to the new-invented method of book-keeping, by Jones; as they comprize, *in one view,* the debits, credits, and other transactions, during a biennial service as *overseer* of Manchester, " ALL IN THE COMPASS OF A CARD !"

I intended to conclude by giving some little information relative to the expences at the New Bayley, but not having had an opportunity of getting even a sight of these accounts, I shall content myself by making a few remarks on *one day's proceedings,* the particulars of which I published, page 18, in my Reply to Mr. Unite.

New-Bayley Court-House, February 6th, 1793.

In this day's charges there appear no less than *thirteen examinations* and *removal orders,* at *nine shillings* each, amounting to five pounds seventeen shillings ; but of late the prices have risen more than *fifty per cent.* There is now an additional *five shillings* paid for " MOVING THE BENCH"— which makes a difference in this day's business, in two items *only,* of three pounds five shillings. There are likewise charged *four vagrant passes,* twelve shillings ; *three warrants,* twelve shillings ; *twenty-three summonses,* one pound three shillings; and six permit passes, six shillings.

As the vagrant passes, and expences in the removals, prosecutions of felons, &c. are defrayed by the county, with which there should be a debtor

and

and creditor account kept, and which ought to make a complete balance.

As the town is charged with twenty-three summonses, at one shilling each, where is the credit given? It being a general rule for the person summoned to pay one shilling, with sixpence for the service;—warrants are also charged to the town, though paid for, in the same manner. The beadles charge Mr. Unite with receiving this money, and even their perquisite for the service. *Passes,* which are numerous in the course of the year, were formerly filled up from printed forms, by the deputy-constable, and the paupers were taken before a magistrate, for his signature, when he might exercise his own discretion;—but of late, they have been *purchased* by the OVERSEERS from the JUSTICES' CLERKS, at *twenty shillings* the SCORE, with the magistrate's signature in BLANK * !

The account of these charges at the New Bayley, amount to £9. 7s. which is *cast up* in the books, £10. 1s. an error on the *right side as usual* of fourteen shillings. I do not wonder at these kind of mistakes, for exclusive of the over-charge itself, it serves to *increase* the discount, as the *overseers* are allowed, by the *justices' clerks,* five per cent. on the amount of *each* day's proceedings, for cash *paid to them* while in *court,* and which discount is generally applied in aid of the very heavy expences attendant on nocturnal mirth, after the *fatigues of the day, instead of appearing to the credit of the town.*

I shall now conclude this publication, by making some few remarks which suggested themselves on reading the interrogatories in the *Manchester Gazette* of this day.

In my Reply to Mr. Unite, twelve months ago, page

* This may be called—*a wholesale kind of justice*—a kind of dealing in the *raw material,* and not to be met with in the *loom of common honesty.*

page 20, I made some observations on the irregularity of Mr. Wharmby's conduct, as *collector*—and of his books being, at that time, in a very confused state. And about six months afterwards the following paragraph appeared in the Chester paper.

" *An accountant, of the first respectability in that* " *profession, has made an offer to inspect the accounts* " *of the police and poor-rates of Manchester, in their* " *present* CONFUSED STATE, *for an allowance of* " *five per cent.,* on CASH RECEIVED, *and by* MIS-" TAKE.*unentered,*" &c. &c.

Had this proposal been accepted, the *collector's books* might, at this time, been fairly balanced, and there would have been a saving of ninety-five pounds per cent. on all the *unentered* cash received, being fairly pointed out; instead of which, an *enormous* POOR RATE has been made on the inhabitants, within these few days, amounting to EIGHTEEN THOUSAND POUNDS!— though so *many* thousand pounds remain yet *uncollected.*

But—will the record gain credit, when it is read, that Mr. Wharmby has *collected taxes* nearly to the amount of FIFTY THOUSAND POUNDS! and that there remain uncollected near TWENTY THOUSAND POUNDS, and that no conclusive settlement of his books has taken place for these last SEVEN YEARS! and still Mr. Wharmby, as collector, keeps his office! at a time when every thing around him " *like the centre of a whirlpool, rolls in confusion.*"

The irregularities in assessments have been numerous, and claim immediate attention. I have known property in the town of Manchester, belonging to an individual, exceeding six hundred pounds per annum, only rated at thirty pounds.— The property of a gentleman, in the centre of the town, whose rental exceeded two hundred and

eighty

eighty pounds, was not applied to for POOR RATES
for *many years*, and it was afterwards *compromised*
by *Mr. Wharmby*, for fourteen pounds, which did
not amount to SEVEN-PENCE in the pound. It is
notorious, that houses belonging to particular individuals, were *not assessed for many years ;* but no
sooner was the property tranferred by sale, than
the purchaser was, in point of taxation, put in
equality with his neighbours. The *partial* and
unjust methods used in *collecting*, equals that of
assessing ; there are many persons of considerable
property, whose taxes have been unpaid for many
years. I have known instances of several notes
being left in the course of a few days, for the *same
rate*, each note differing *very considerably* in amount;
and it likewise may appear rather unaccountable,
that the collector *very often* makes a demand of a
particular sum of money, and afterwards reduces
it to *one-half* of his original claim.

The collector, Mr. Wharmby, a few weeks ago,
called on Mr. Hammond, the Star Inn, Dean's-
gate, and demanded FIVE POUNDS for *highway
composition money*—but before he left the house, he
gave Mr. H. a RECEIPT IN FULL ON RECEIVING
THREE POUNDS—must not this demand have been
made for more than the sum specified in his books?
—for *no* collector has a power to alter a BOOK OF
RATES, after it is signed by the magistrates. Mr.
Hammond, having got the receipt for THREE
POUNDS, very facetiously observed to a friend,
" *If* I had paid *Mr. Wharmby the five pounds, which
he at first charged, what would have become of the*
FORTY SHILLINGS *which he afterwards abated ?*"

Such of my readers who peruse these pages with
candour and impartiality, I trust will allow that
the present mode of publication, is the only means
left in my power to bring these charges before the

public, and which were intended to have been brought forward at a public meeting, *sanctioned* at *that* time by the boroughreeve and constables—but who afterwards declined countenancing the same, on the most *simple* and *paltry plea*, as mentioned in the 4th page of this publication.

It appears but too evident, that the boroughreeve and constables—are wholly bent on keeping " *things as they are*;" but they are attempting that which is in its nature impossible.

When the most *flagrant* acts of *cruel* and *unjust* proceedings are known to exist, and conviction shall have taken place—no screen—no subterfuge —will impose so far on the judgment of the public, as to fascinate their discernment, and lead them tamely to submit to be the dupes of *official confederacy.*

I am by no means ignorant of the false motives which, from various causes, have been attributed to my conduct on the subject of the foregoing pages; —I again repeat, what I asserted in the commencement of this publication, that no *political* or *party* spirit (every idea of which I disclaim) has had, even the smallest share, in this transaction; and I trust it will also be allowed, that interest forms no part of my views, when I declare, that I am a very considerable loser—both by the time I have dedicated to, and the expences which I have incurred in the procuring the necessary information on the subject.

No apology will, I trust, be deemed necessary by those to whom these pages are addressed, for the extraordinary length to which they have unavoidably been extended.—If I have trespassed on the attention of my reader, it has been with a view to *elucidate* and *explain*;—if I have any where warmly expressed an indignant feeling—I trust the occasion

sion has justified the language ;—if I have erred in
any manner, it has been in judgment, and not in
motive ;—therefore, as I have had no private pique
to gratify—no partial interest to promote—I rely
on the candour of my readers—to *acquit* or *con-
demn*—having acted solely from an earnest wish to
do a—*public good.*

As

As it has been the uniform practice, for a *long* series of years, for the deputy constable to *issue precepts* to the constables of the surrounding hamlets, and to *receive* the *county rates*, which have, in many parishes, *exceeded* their *poor rates*,—and the deputy constable being of late restrained from receiving the same, by circular orders, directing such monies to be paid to the *head* constables—gave so general an alarm, that I thought it not only my duty to publish the following statement, for the *future* government of the surrounding constables— but, that it may lead to detection of any *past* extortion ; and which may be *easily* proved by a reference to the *money warrants*, and the following calculation :

A PERFECT CALCULATION OF COUNTY RATES.

When any sum of money is charged upon the COUNTY OF LANCASTER, betwixt *one pound* and *one thousand*, this calculation gives a true account what sum is to be paid by *every* HUNDRED within the said *county*.

It also points out the proportionate share of every township in the Hundred of Salford, betwixt TEN SHILLINGS and ONE HUNDRED POUNDS.

Also, gives an exact account of the monies paid, for the above rates, by the *eleven* villages under the Township of Manchester.

When the County of Lancaster is charged with any of the undermentioned Sums,

	£. 1000	£. 500	£. 200	£. 100	£. 50			£. 20			£. 10			£. 5			£. 2			£. 1		
the several Hundreds therein pay as follow:	£.	£.	£.	£.	£.	s.	d.	£.	s.	d.	£.	s.	d.	£.	s.	d.	£.	s.	d.	£.	s.	d.
Derby Hundred . .	240	120	48	24	12	0	0	4	16	0	2	8	0	1	4	0	0	9	7¼	0	4	9½
Salford Do.	140	70	28	14	7	0	0	2	16	0	1	8	0	0	14	0	0	5	7¼	0	2	9¼
Leyland Do.	90	45	18	9	4	10	0	1	16	0	0	18	0	0	9	0	0	3	7¼	0	1	9½
Blackburn Do. . . .	180	90	36	18	9	0	0	3	12	0	1	16	0	0	18	0	0	7	2½	0	3	7¼
Amownderness Do.	190	95	38	19	9	10	0	3	16	0	1	18	0	0	19	0	0	7	7¼	0	3	9½
Lonsdall Do.	160	80	32	16	8	0	0	3	4	0	1	12	0	0	16	0	0	6	4¾	0	3	2½

When the Hundred of Salford is charged with any of the follow sums, the several Townships therein pay as follow;

	£100			£60			£26			£10			£5			£2			£1			10		
Manchester	9	3	11¼	4	11	11¼	1	16	9¼	0	18	4¼	0	9	2¼	0	3	8¼	0	1	10	0	0	11
Salford	3	1	3¼	1	10	7¼	0	12	3¼	0	6	1¼	0	3	¾	0	1	2¼	0	0	7¼	0	0	3¼
Stratford	1	4	6¼	0	12	3¼	0	4	11	0	2	5½	0	1	2¾	0	0	6	0	0	3	0	0	1½
Withington	5	4	3	2	12	3	0	1	1	0	10½		0	5¼		0	2	1	0	1		0	0	6½
Heaton Norris	1	16	9¼	0	18	4¼	0	7	7	0	3	8¾	0	1	10½	0	0	9	0	0	4½	0	0	2¼
Chorlton	0	12	3½	0	6	1½	0	2	5½	0	1	2¾	0	7¼		0	0	3	0	0	1½	0	0	¾
Raddish	1	10	8	0	15	5	0	6	4½	0	3	1	0	1	6½	0	0	7½	0	0	3¾	0	0	1¾
Cheetham	0	11	3½	0	5	7¼	0	2	3	0	1	1½	0	6¾		0	0	2¾	0	0	1½	0	0	1
Worsley	2	18	2¼	0	9	7¼	0	11	7½	0	5	10	0	2	11	0	1	2	0	0	7	0	0	3½
Clifton	0	18	4¼	0	9	2¼	0	3	8¼	0	1	10	0	11		0	0	4½	0	0	2¼	0	0	1
Barton	3	19	8¼	0	19	10¼	0	15	11	0	7	11½	0	4		0	1	7	0	0	9½	0	0	4½
Pendleton	1	16	9¼	0	18	4¼	0	7	4½	0	3	8	0	1	10	0	0	9	0	0	4½	0	0	2¼
Pendlebury	0	10	2¼	0	5	1½	0	2	0½	0	1	0¼	0	6		0	0	2½	0	0	1¼	0	0	¾
Urmston	0		6¼	0	5		0	4	1¾	0	3½		0	2¼		0	0	1	0	0	¾	0	0	¼
Flixton	4	2	11	0	5½		0	8	7	0	4	1¾	0	2	4¼	0	0	11¼	0	0	4¼	0	0	2¼
Preswich	2	12	1¼	0	6	0¼	0	10	5¾	0	5	2¾	0	2	7¼	0	1	0¾	0	0	6¼	0	0	3
Pilkington	2	12	1½	0	6	0¼	0	10	5¼	0	5	2¾	0	2	7¼	0	1	0¾	0	0	6¼	0	0	3
Middleton	5	16	1¼	0	2	18	0	3	2¾	0	7½		0	3¾		0	1	7½	0	0	9¼	0	0	¾
Asheton	5	16		0	2	18	0	2	3¼	0	11		0	5		0	2	3¾	0	1	2	0	0	7
Hundersfield	4	7	4¼	2	3	8	0	3	4	0	11	7½	0	5	9¾	0	2	3½	0	1		0	10¼	
Castleton	1	18		2	3		0	17	5½	0	8	9	0	4		0	2	3½	0	1	2	0	3½	

Spotland 2	18	0	0	0	1	11	2	0	9¼	5	7¼	11	0	0	1	3¼
Butterworth 2	18	0	0	0	1	11	2	0	9¼	5	7¼	11	0	0	1	3½
Oldham ....:	18	8	0	7	0	11	1	0	9½	3	8¼	7	0	0	0	2¼
Royton .:.........0	19	4	0	7	0	11¼	0	0	10¼	1	10¼	3	0	8	4	1¼
Chadderton 1	9	0	0	4½	0	5¼	1	0	11½	2	9¼	5	6	9	1	1¼
Crompton 1	9	0	0	3¼	0	5½	1	0	10¼	2	9¾	5	6	9	1¾
Bolton 1	14	1½	0	4	0	8¼	1	0	10¼	3	9½	6	0¾	14	2
Turton and Long-																
worth 1	14	1½	0	4	0	8¼	1	0	5	3	0:10	6	0¼	17	4
Edgworth & Ham-																
blets...........1	14	1¼	0	4	0	8¼	1	0	5	3	6	10	0¼	17	4
Blackrod & Aspull:1	14	1½	0	4	0	8¼	1	0	5	3	6	10	0¼	17	4
Rivington, Lostock,																
and Anlerarph..:1	14	1½	0	4	0	8¼	1	0	5	3	6	10	0¼	17	4
Three Hiltons......1	14	1½	0	4	0	8¾	1	0	5	3	6	10	0¼	17	4
Westhoughton 1	14	1½	0	4	0	8¼	1	0	5	3	6	10	0¼	17	4
Farnworth, Rum-																
worth, & Kersley	14	1½	0	4	0	8¼	1	0	5	3	6	10	0¼	17	4
Heaton, Horridge,																
and Halliwell....1	14	1¼	0	4	0	8¼	1	0	5	3	6	10	0¼	17	4
Radcliff...........1	14	1½	0	4	0	8½	1	0	5	3	6	10	0¼	17	4
Bury 6	16	5½	3	2¼	6:10	7¼	6	13	7¼	13	2½	8	8½	8
Tottington 3	8	2½	1½	1½	7¾	5¼	3	10	6	14	1½	4¼
Harwood Hamblets.1	14	1½	0	0	0	8¼	1	0	5	3	6	10	0¼	17	0

When the eleven Townships under Manchester are charged with any of the following Sums, the several Townships pay as follow;

	£100.	£50.	£20.	£10.	£5.	£2.	£1.	10s.	5s.
Bradford..	3 6 8	1 13 4	0 13 4	0 6 8	0 3 4	0 1 4	0 0 8	0 0 4	0 0 2
Harpurhey	3 6 8	1 13 4	0 13 4	0 6 8	0 3 4	0 1 4	0 0 8	0 0 4	0 0 2
Hulme ...	3 19 2	1 19 7	0 15 10	0 7 11	0 3 11¼	0 1 7	0 0 9½	0 0 4	0 0 2½
Openshaw	6 13 4	3 6 8	1 6 8	0 13 4	0 6 8	0 2 8	0 1 4	0 0 8	0 0 4
Ardwick..	6 13 4	3 6 8	1 6 8	0 13 4	0 6 8	0 2 8	0 1 4	0 0 8	0 0 4
Crumpsall	10 16 8	5 8 4	2 3 4	1 1 8	0 10 10	0 4 4	0 2 2	0 1 1	0 0 6¼
Droysden	10 16 8	5 8 4	2 3 4	1 1 8	0 10 10	0 4 4	0 2 2	0 1 1	0 0 6¼
Gorton ...	12 10 0	6 5 0	2 10 0	1 5 0	0 12 6	0 5 0	0 2 6	0 1 3	0 0 7½
Failsworth	12 10 0	6 5 0	2 10 0	1 5 0	0 12 6	0 5 0	0 2 6	0 1 3	0 0 7½
Blakeley..	14 7 0	7 3 9	2 17 0	1 8 9	0 14 4½	0 5 9	0 2 10½	0 1 5½	0 0 8¼
Newton ...	15 0 0	7 10 0	3 0 0	1 10 0	0 15 0	0 6 0	0 3 0	0 1 6	0 0 9

When the Constables of Manchester are charged by the *County* or *Hundred*, with any Sum of Money, as a County Rate, the *eleven* Townships pay collectively TWO-THIRDS of the Sum—whose Proportions of a Pound, are as follow:

Bradford, 8d. ——Harpurhey, 8d.——Hulme, 9¼d. ——Openshaw, 1s. 4d.——Ardwick, 1s. 4d.
Droylsden, 2s. 2d.——Crumpsall, 2s. 2d.——Gorton, 2s. 6d.——Failsworth, 2s. 6d.——Blakley, 2s. 10½d.
Newton, 3s.

ACKNOWLEDGEMENTS TO CORRESPONDENTS.

P. S—'s account, *relative to Mr. Unite's journey to Vale-Royal, to demand a reward of one hundred pounds for the apprehension of a* felon—*the falsehoods he made use of to T. Cholmondeley and T. B. Bayley, Esqrs.—his method of taking the thief —and of his being* TWICE STABBED, *&c. appear from the testimony of Mr. Harry Woodhouse and Mr. Eph. Rowbottom—like Jack Falstaff's story,—nine men in buckram ;—as Mr. Unite was not present at the time when the felon was apprehended, and never saw him till he was taken by the above gentlemen to the police-office, &c. were I to have detailed all the relations of this nature, this publication might have rivalled, in point of bulk, the* statutes at large.

R——d's *complaint against a special constable, a Mr. C——, who appears to be armed with power for the very basest of purposes, has little to do with the disclosure of parochial abuses—yet, it is an abuse of that nature, which, if properly substantiated, T. B. as the friend of order, cannot reject noticing.*

M—— *ought to have preferred a bill of indictment at the present quarter sessions, if what he relates be* true---no doubt, *but the present grand jury would have found a bill* against the party.

X. X. *will be attended to.*

Veritas's *communications may be perfectly true, but he should have sent his real signature, respecting the stolen goods. The account given by V—, of Mr. Unite's reporting to Justice Bayley, that there was a seditious meeting, at the Star Inn, Dean's-gate—Mr. B. himself found on enquiry at the inn, that the report of Mr. Unite was entirely a fabrication of his own—the meeting only consisted of five persons on business of arbitration.*

A "*Flagellator's lash*" *would perhaps be more wholesomely applied to the* back *than the* book—*in which case, if Flagellator had not the merit of making an* honest, *he would at least make a* smart *overseer.*

Mr. Williams's (overseer of Warrington) five letters, and account current, cannot be noticed—Mr. Hallows not having yet delivered in his accounts for the year 1794.

* * * *'s *very pathetic account of the cruel treatment of a young woman, who was forced to the New Bayley prison by a* special constable, without a warrant, *and* without her having committed

committed any offence *(save that of being pregnant, and belonging to another parish) shall soon make its appearance, for the sake of humanity, as well as public justice. The forcing her from her dwelling, late in the evening, with the ill treatment she received, threw her into violent labour pains, and in that pitiful situation she continued all night in prison, without a bed—the following morning she was dragged away to Mr. Paynter's office, where violent fits of labour continuing, she begged permission to go into the yard—a few minutes afterwards she was found in the* necessary *delivered of a* dead child!

＊＊＊＊ *'s account given of Hallows and his wife's inhuman treatment to a poor woman and her infant, about five weeks old, I can rely upon :—this shall also present itself to the public eye.*